Go for it!

BOOK 1

DAVID NUNAN

HEINLE & HEINLE

—— ★ ——
™

THOMSON LEARNING

The publication of *Go for it!* was directed by members of the Newbury House ESL/EFL team at Heinle & Heinle:

    Erik Gundersen, Editorial Director
    Amy Terrell, International Marketing Manager
    Maryellen Killeen, Production Services Coordinator
    Nancy Mann Jordan, Senior Developmental Editor
    Thomas Healy, Developmental Editor
    Stanley J. Galek, Vice President and Publisher

Also participating in the publication of this program were:

    Evelyn Nelson, Director of Global ELT Training
      and Development
    Charlotte Sturdy, Market Development Director
    Tom Dare, Market Development Director
    Amy Lawler, Managing Developmental Editor
    Mary Sutton, Associate Market Development Director
    Mary Beth Hennebury, Manufacturing Coordinator
    Elise Kaiser, Production Manager
    Rollins Design and Production,
      page design and production management
    Ha Nguyen Design, cover designer
    Jeff Dinardo Design, interior design
    Pre-Press Company Inc., composition and pre-press
    Martha Friedman, art coordination
    Janet McCartney, proofreading and indexing
    Tab Hamlin, copyediting
    Jim Carson, Dick Daniels, Tim Haggerty, Fran O'Neil,
      Terry Sirrell, Bob Staake, illustrators
    Jonathan Stark, Image Resources Director
    Deborah Gordon, John Chapman, contributors

Printed in Canada

ISBN 0-8384-6773-3

10 9 8 7 6 5

Acknowledgments

I would like to thank all those who have helped shape this project. Particular thanks go to Erik Gundersen, who helped me through the tough times, to Amy Terrell, Maryellen Killeen, Evelyn Nelson, Stan Galek and Charlie Heinle.

In addition, I wish to thank the various International Thomson Publishing personnel who provided input and advice. Special mention must be made of the contribution made by Karen Chiang and her team at ITP (Asia), and Bruno Paul and Francisco Lozano at International Thomson Editores. I would also like to acknowledge and thank Ken Keobke for his critical review of early drafts of the materials.

Above all, thanks must go to my editors Nancy Jordan and Thomas Healy for their dedication to this project. Their commitment of time and critical review went well beyond what any author could hope for or expect.

David Nunan

The author and publisher would like to thank the following individuals who offered many helpful insight, ideas, and suggestions for change during the development of Go for it!

- Vera Andre de Almeida, Instituto Cultural Brasil-Estados Unidos, Rio de Janeiro
- Lucia de Aragão, União Cultural Brasil-Estados Unidos, Sao Paulo
- Jennifer Bixby, Acton, Massachusetts
- Lucia Santos, Casa Thomas Jefferson, Brasilia
- Elizabeth Rabello, Casa Thomas Jefferson, Brasilia
- Marta Diniz, Casa Thomas Jefferson, Brasilia
- Walkiria Darahem, Associacão Cultural Brasil-Estados Unidos, Riberão Preto
- Marilyn Bach, Bronx Public Schools, New York
- David Bohlke, Sejong University Language Research Institute, Seoul
- Wendy Brooks, YBM Si-Sa-young-O-Sa, Seoul
- Dr. Melvin Clark, ClarkHeller Education Center, San Juan, Texas
- Mary Corbin, Manatee County Public Schools, Florida
- Katy Cox, Casa Thomas Jefferson, Brasilia
- Nanette Dougherty, Richmond Hills High School, Queens, New York
- Jo Fritschel, San Diego City Schools, California
- Alejandra Gallegos, Interlingua Aguascalientes, Mexico
- Angie Ginty, District 15, Brooklyn, New York
- Raquel de Gomez, Instituto Culturale Mexicano-Norte Americano de Jalisco, Jalisco
- Carol C.H. Feng, Taipei
- Anne-Marie Hadzima, National Taiwan University, Taipei
- Hui-wen Huang, YMCA, Taipei
- Seung Eun Kang, YBM Si-Sa-young-O-Sa, Seoul
- Jennifer Kellie, AEON, Okayama
- Sung Mi Kim, YBM Si-Sa-young-O-Sa, Seoul
- Athina Leite, ACBEU, Salvador
- Claudina Lo Valvo, Instituto Cultural Argentino, Buenos Aires
- Peter Oram, So Jung Middle School, Dong-gu
- Mary Riggs, Simi Valley USD, California
- Joyce Chin Shao, The Language Training and Testing Center, Taipei
- Stephen Sloan, James Monroe High School, Los Angeles, California
- John Alan Smith, Owada High School, Osaka
- Claudia Spelman, Conejo Valley USD, California
- Barbara Tedesco, Roselle Board of Education, New Jersey
- Lilian Vaisman, Instituto Cultural Brasil-Estados Unidos, Rio de Janeiro
- Maria Vasquez, San Marcos ISD, Texas

Go for it! Book 1: Contents

Target language	Vocabulary	Recycling
What's your name? My name is Gina. I'm Gina. Nice to meet you. What's your phone number? It's 284-2942.	personal names numbers 0-9 phone number first name, last name Hi, Hello	
Is this your pencil? Yes, it is. No, it isn't. What's this in English? It's a pencil. How do you spell pencil?	the alphabet pencil, pen, book, eraser, ruler, pencil case, backpack, ID card, baseball, watch, key, computer game, notebook, ring	your, his, her names numbers 0-9
This is my brother. Is she your sister? Yes, she is. No, she isn't.	mother, father, sister, brother, grandmother, grandfather, friend, grandparents, uncle, aunt, cousin, parents	Hello. Hi. Nice to meet you. personal names Is this your . . .? Yes, it is. Is that your . . .? No, it isn't.
Where's my backpack? It's under the bed. Are my books on the chair? No they're not. I don't know.	table, bed, dresser, bookcase, sofa, chair, backpack, CD, alarm clock, math book, video cassette, hat	keys, books, baseball, computer game, pencil case, ruler, notebook, pen, pencil, ID card Is it . . .? Yes, it is. No, it isn't.
Do you have a basketball? Yes, I do. Let's watch TV. No, that sounds boring. That sounds great.	TV, ball, basketball, soccer, bat, tennis racket, volleyball, interesting, boring, fun, difficult, relaxing	I, you, he, she baseball, computer game, sister numbers 0-9 personal names
Do you like hamburgers? Yes, I do. No, I don't. I like french fries. I don't like tomatoes.	hamburgers, tomatoes, broccoli, french fries, oranges, ice cream, salad, bananas, eggs, carrots, apples, chicken breakfast, lunch, dinner fruit, vegetable	Let's I, you, he, she personal names
How much is the blue T-shirt? It's 10 dollars. Ok, I'll take it. Thank you. You're welcome.	socks, T-shirt, pants, shorts, sweater, bag, dollars black, white, green, red, blue numbers 10-31	hat I like . . . Do you like . . .? Do you have . . .? numbers 1-9

Go for it! Book 1: Contents

Target language	Vocabulary	Recycling
When is your birthday? My birthday is November 11th. When is Sarah's birthday? Sarah's birthday is January 21st. How old are you? I'm thirteen.	months of the year ordinal numbers 1st–31st birthday, party, speech contest, school trip	basketball, game, volleyball his, her
Do you want to go to a movie? Yes, I do. I want to go to an action movie. What kind of movies do you like? I like action movies and thrillers, but I don't like romances.	action movie, romance, thriller, comedy fun, great, scary, funny, exciting, sad	I like . . . She doesn't like . . . boring
Can you dance? Yes, I can. No, I can't. What club do you want to join? I want to join the music club. I can't sing. What can you do? I can dance.	dance, swim, sing, play chess, paint, speak Spanish, play the guitar, art, music, guitar, drums, piano, trumpet, violin	Do you like . . . ? I like . . . I don't like . . . Let's basketball, baseball
What time do you usually get up? I get up at six o'clock. When does Alicia take a shower? She takes a shower at five o'clock. What time is it? It's eleven o'clock.	get up, run, eat breakfast, go to school, eat dinner, do homework, go to bed, shower, o'clock morning, afternoon, evening usually, pen pal	numbers 1–30
What's your favorite subject? My favorite subject is P.E. Why do you like P.E.? Because it's fun. Who is your math teacher? Mrs. O'Sullivan.	math, science, history, physical education (P.E.) favorite, teacher days of the week	interesting, relaxing, difficult, exciting, fun, boring lunch time expressions music, art numbers 1–12 I have . . . Do you like . . . ? When do you . . . ?
Where is your pen pal from? She's from Mexico. Where does she live? She lives in Mexico City. What language does she speak? She speaks English and Spanish.	Taiwan, Korea, Japan, The United States, Brazil, Australia, The United Kingdom, Mexico, Argentina English, Spanish, Chinese, Portuguese, Japanese, Korean	She has . . . brothers, sisters What's her name? P.E., music, movies, pen pal

Go for it! Book 1: Contents

Target language	Vocabulary	Recycling
What are you doing? I'm doing my homework. Do you want to go swimming? Yes, I do. When do you want to go? At three o' clock.	watching, doing, eating cleaning, playing, swimming, shopping, reading pool, school, mall, library	Do you want . . . ? Let's . . . boring, interesting time expressions
Is there a bank near here? Yes, there's a bank on Center Street. Where's the supermarket? It's next to the library. Is there a pay phone in the neighborhood? Yes, it's on Bridge Street on the right.	post office, hotel, video arcade, bank, supermarket, street, pay phone, park new, clean, quiet, big, small, dirty, old, busy left, right next to, across from near, between	What are you doing? Do you want to . . . ?
Why do you like koala bears? Because they are cute. They're kind of shy. They're very big.	tiger, elephant, koala bear, dolphin, panda, lion, penguin, giraffe smart, cute, ugly, intelligent, friendly, beautiful, shy, kind of, very Africa, China	friendly, fun, small Australia, Japan, Brazil He is from . . . She's five years old. quiet, scary, interesting

Guide to Go for it!

There are six pages in every unit of the Go for it! series. Each unit consists of two lessons (A and B) and a self check. Use this annotated unit to discover how Go for it! will develop your students' ability to communicate confidently in English from the very first day!

In Go for it! new language builds upon recycled language in a natural, gradual way:

Lesson A provides step-by-step presentation and guided practice of the target language.

Lesson B gets students to use the language to complete tasks in more open-ended and creative ways.

The **Self Check** allows students to confirm the English they have learned.

• **Language Goals** focus students' learning.

• Built-in **picture dictionary** introduces key vocabulary.

• **Speech bubbles** provide clear models of target functions.

• Easy-to-complete **listening task** gives students an immediate feeling of accomplishment.

• **Guided speaking activity** gets students to produce target language from the beginning.

2a Listen and circle the foods you hear.

hamburgers   tomatoes   broccoli   french fries
oranges   ice cream   salad   bananas

2b Listen again and fill in the blanks.

I like **1.** hamburgers.
Do you like **2.** hamburgers?

Yes, I do.

Do you like
3. _____?

No, I don't like
4. _____.

Let's have
5. _____.   Oh, no.

No?   I don't like
6. _____.

2c   PAIRWORK

Practice the conversation above. Give answers that are true for you.

Grammar Focus

Do you like salad?	Yes, I do.	No, I don't.
Do they like salad?	Yes, they do.	No, they don't.
Does he like salad?	Yes, he does.	No, he doesn't.
Does she like salad?	Yes, she does.	No, she doesn't.

I like oranges.	I don't like bananas.
They like salad.	They don't like broccoli.
He likes hamburgers.	He doesn't like french fries.
She likes ice cream.	She doesn't like bananas.

32 UNIT 6 • Do you like bananas?

- **Frequent listenings** develop students' ability to comprehend natural language.

- **Pair work** provides frequent opportunities for personalization.

- **Grammar focus** highlights the unit's key structures.

- **Activities** including information gaps and games provide opportunities for dynamic classroom interaction.

3   PAIRWORK

Student A looks at this page.
Student B looks at page 99.
Ask your partner questions.
Find out what Bill and Bob
like and don't like.

Draw ☺ or ☹ in the chart.

Bob   Bill

Chart for Student A.

	🍟	🍅	🥗	🍲
Bob	☺		☹	☺
Bill		☹		☺

4   GAME Do You Like...?

Go around the class. Find students who
like these things. Write their names on
the picture. The first person to write
a name on each food is a winner.

Does Bob
like tomatoes?   No, he doesn't.

Jill, do you
like tomatoes?   No, I don't.

We like
tomatoes!

UNIT 6 • Do you like bananas? **33**

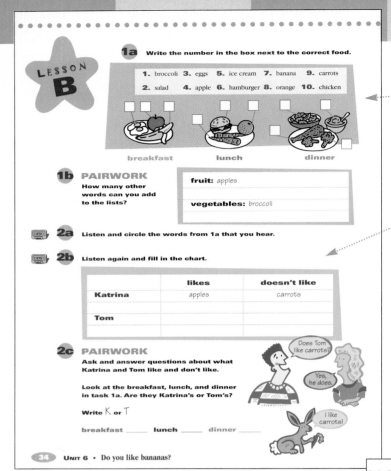

1a Write the number in the box next to the correct food.

1. broccoli 3. eggs 5. ice cream 7. banana 9. carrots
2. salad 4. apple 6. hamburger 8. orange 10. chicken

breakfast   lunch   dinner

1b PAIRWORK
How many other words can you add to the lists?

fruit: apples

vegetables: broccoli

2a Listen and circle the words from 1a that you hear.

2b Listen again and fill in the chart.

	likes	doesn't like
Katrina	apples	carrots
Tom		

2c PAIRWORK
Ask and answer questions about what Katrina and Tom like and don't like.

Look at the breakfast, lunch, and dinner in task 1a. Are they Katrina's or Tom's?

Write K or T

breakfast _____ lunch _____ dinner _____

Does Tom like carrots?

Yes, he does.

I like carrots!

- **Vocabulary expansion** increases students' ability to converse about the topic.

- **Natural listenings** integrate new language with language introduced in earlier units.

- **Realistic yet level-appropriate readings** develop students' skills through a variety of reading strategies.

- **Gradual progression** from reading to writing builds students' confidence in their writing ability.

- **Final activity** gets students to activate the unit's language in creative, open-ended ways.

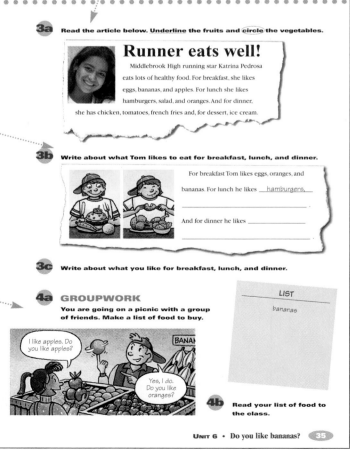

3a Read the article below. Underline the fruits and circle the vegetables.

Runner eats well!

Middlebrook High running star Katrina Pedrosa eats lots of healthy food. For breakfast, she likes eggs, bananas, and apples. For lunch she likes hamburgers, salad, and oranges. And for dinner, she has chicken, tomatoes, french fries and, for dessert, ice cream.

3b Write about what Tom likes to eat for breakfast, lunch, and dinner.

For breakfast Tom likes eggs, oranges, and bananas. For lunch he likes ___hamburgers,___

_____

And for dinner he likes _____

_____

3c Write about what you like for breakfast, lunch, and dinner.

4a GROUPWORK
You are going on a picnic with a group of friends. Make a list of food to buy.

LIST

bananas

I like apples. Do you like apples?

Yes, I do. Do you like oranges?

BANA

4b Read your list of food to the class.

- **Self Check** activities motivate students by showing them what they have learned.

- **Vocabulary builder** at the back of the book encourages students to keep a learning log of the words they know.

- **Humorous cartoons** that use the target language help to make learning fun!

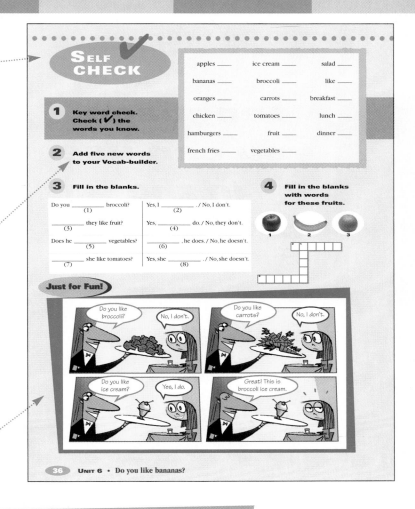

The complete *Go for it!* **package includes many opportunities for additional practice of each unit's language focus.**

Language you can use in the classroom!

LESSON A

My name's Gina.

 1a

Listen and number the conversations [1–3] in the picture.

Language Goals: Introduce yourself, Greet people

My name's Jenny.

I'm Gina. Nice to meet you.

What's your name?

Hello. I'm Mary.

Hi, Mary. I'm Jim.

1

Francisco.

LOST & FOUND

TRASH

1b PAIRWORK

Practice the conversations in the picture.

1c Now meet the other students in the class.

What's your name?

My name's _____.

2a Listen to the two conversations and number the pictures [1–2].

2b Listen again and complete the conversations with the words in the box.

I'm	is	name	name
name's	his	✔ your	

Conversation 1

Tony: Hello. What's ___your___ name?
(1)

Jenny: My __name is__ Jenny.
(2)

Tony: _____ Tony.
(3)

Jenny: Nice to meet you, Tony.

Conversation 2

Bill: What's _____ name?
(4)

Maria: His _____ is Tony.
(5)

Bill: And what's her _____ ?
(6)

Maria: Her name _____ Jenny.
(7)

2c PAIRWORK

Practice Conversation 1. Use your own names.

Questions	Answers	Look!
What's your name?	My name's Jenny.	What's = What is
	I'm Jenny.	I'm = I am
What's his name?	His name's Tony.	name's = name is
What's her name?	Her name's Gina.	

3a Draw a line from each name to *First Name* or *Last Name*.

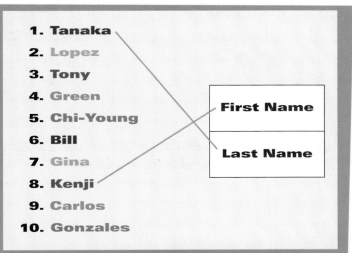

1. Tanaka
2. Lopez
3. Tony
4. Green
5. Chi-Young
6. Bill
7. Gina
8. Kenji
9. Carlos
10. Gonzales

First Name

Last Name

3b Ask your classmates their first names and last names. Make a list.

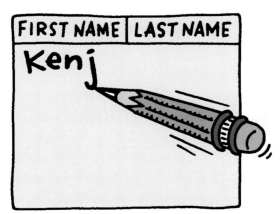

4 Name Game
GROUPWORK
Play the name game.

 1a Listen and repeat.

0 "oh"	**2** two	**4** four	**6** six	**8** eight
1 one	**3** three	**5** five	**7** seven	**9** nine

 1b Listen to the conversation. Listen again and write the telephone number.

___ ___ ___ - ___ ___ ___ ___

 1c GROUPWORK

Ask for and tell your phone numbers.

What's your phone number, Kim?

It's 281-9176.

 2a Listen and match the names and telephone numbers.

1. Alfonso ___c___   a. 929-31 __ __

2. Rita _____   b. 398-61 __ __

3. James _____   c. 278-79 __ __

4. Mary _____   d. 555-80 __ __

 2b Listen again and complete the phone numbers.

 2c Ask four classmates their phone numbers and fill in the address book.

Names	Phone Numbers

3a Look at the picture. Find the last names and write them below.

1. Karen _Suarez_

2. Kenji _____

3. Chi-Young _____

4. Jim _____

5. Maria _____

3b Fill in an ID card for Tanya.

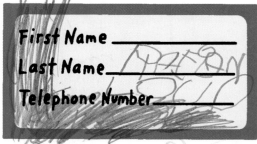

First Name _____

Last Name _____

Telephone Number _____

My name is Tanya Lopez. My phone number is 535-2375.

3c Fill in your own ID card.

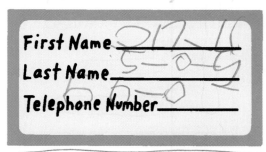

First Name _____

Last Name _____

Telephone Number _____

4 Write your phone number on a piece of paper and put it in a bag. Then, take a piece of paper and find the owner.

What's your phone number?

SELF CHECK

1 Key word check. Check (✔) the words you know.

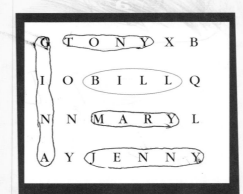

I _own_   it ____   is ____

hi ____   what ____   my ____

Hello ____   your ____   his ____

her ____   first name ____   last name ____

telephone number ____

2 Write five new words in your Vocab-builder.

3 Fill in the blanks with words from this unit.

What __is__ your name?   My __name__ is Jim.
    (1)   (2)

_____ is his name?   His name __is__ Ricardo.
  (3)   (4)

What is __your__ name?   Her __name__ is Gina.
        (5)   (6)

4 Find the names in the box.

✔ Bill   ✔ Gina   ✔ Jenny
✔ Mary   ✔ Tony

G	T O N Y	X	B
I	O	B I L L	Q
N	N	M A R Y	L
A	Y	J E N N Y	

Just for Fun!

PSST!

WHAT'S YOUR FIRST NAME?

ZIG.

WHAT'S YOUR LAST NAME?

ZAG.

LESSON A

Is this your pencil?

1a

Match the words with the things in the picture.

1. pencil __c__

2. pen ____

3. book ____

4. eraser ____

5. ruler ____

6. pencil case ____

7. backpack ____

Language Goal: Identify ownership

1b **Listen and number the conversations [1–3] in the picture above.**

1c **PAIRWORK**

Practice the conversation. Talk about things in the picture.

2a Listen and check (✔) the things you hear.

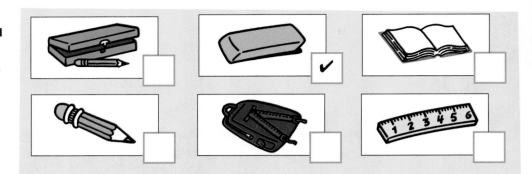

2b Listen and complete the conversation with the words in the box.

| pencil | ruler | ✔ eraser | pencil | ruler |

Teacher: What's this in English?

Tim: Is it an __eraser__ ?
　　　　　　　　　(1)

Teacher: No, it isn't.

Sonia: Is it a _____ ?
　　　　　　　　(2)

Teacher: No, it isn't a _____ .
　　　　　　　　　　　　(3)

Joe: Is it a _____ ?
　　　　　　(4)

Teacher: Yes, it is. Is this your _____ ?
　　　　　　　　　　　　　　　　(5)

Joe: No, it isn't. It's his pencil.

2c **PAIRWORK**

Ask about the things in the picture.

What's this in English?

It's a backpack.

Grammar Focus

Is this your pencil?	Yes, it is.
Is this my pen?	No, it isn't.
Is that his book?	Yes, it is.
Is that her eraser?	No, it isn't.

3a Listen and repeat the letters of the alphabet.

Aa Bb Cc Dd Ee Ff Gg Hh Ii Jj Kk Ll Mm
Nn Oo Pp Qq Rr Ss Tt Uu Vv Ww Xx Yy Zz

3b Practice the conversation. Then make conversations about the pictures below.

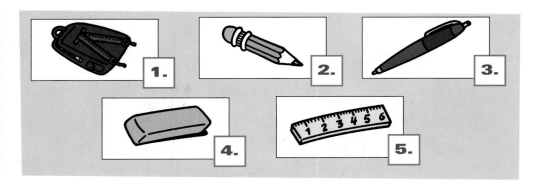

1.

2.

3.

4.

5.

A: What's this in English?

B: It's a pen.

A: How do you spell pen?

B: P-E-N.

4a GAME Find the Owner.

Put something into the teacher's bag.

4b Take something out of the bag and find the owner. You only have two guesses!

Is this your eraser?

No, it isn't.

LESSON B

1a Match the words with the things in the picture.

1. baseball _a_	3. computer game __	5. key __	7. ring __
2. (watch) __	4. ID card __	6. notebook __	8. pen __

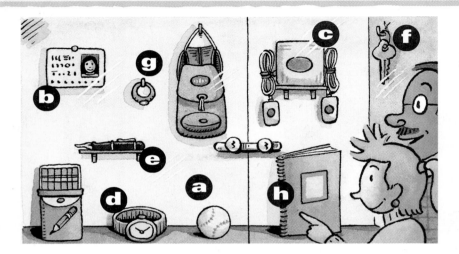

1b PAIRWORK

Ask questions about the things in the picture.

How do you spell watch?

W-A-T-C-H.

2a Listen. Look at the words in activity 1a. Circle the things that you hear.

2b Listen again. Write the things in the chart.

Kelsey	Mike
watch	

2c PAIRWORK

Now ask about other students' things. Student A, look at page 98. Student B, look at page 100.

3a Read the bulletin board notices and (circle) the things from activity 1.

Is this your watch?
Call John at
495-3539.

Francisco,
Is that your computer game
in the lost and found case?

Rick

Found: Gold ring.
Is this your(ring?)
Please call Mary.
Phone # 235-0285.

Lost:
My school ID card.
My name is Steve.
Please call 685-6034.

3b Put these pieces in order to make a message.
Write numbers in the boxes.

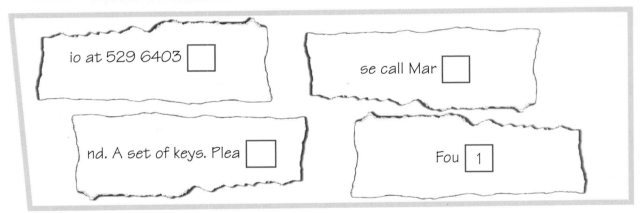

io at 529 6403 ☐

se call Mar ☐

nd. A set of keys. Plea ☐

Fou 1

3c Write your own bulletin board message.

4 GROUPWORK
Draw a picture on the
board. The other students
guess what it is.

What's this?

Is it a watch?

backpack _____	notebook _____	computer game _____
baseball _____	pen _____	ruler _____
book _____	pencil case _____	ID card _____
eraser _____	ring _____	watch _____
key _____	pencil _____	

1 Key word check. Check (✔) the words you know.

2 Write five new words in your Vocab-builder.

3 Fill in the blanks with words from the unit.

_____ that your pencil?
(1)

Is _____ your pen?
(3)

What _____ that in English?
(5)

Yes, it _____ .
(2)

No, it _____ .
(4)

_____ a ruler.
(6)

4 Look at the alphabet chart. What do the numbers spell?

16, 5, 14, 3, 9, 12 = __PENCIL__

18, 21, 12, 5, 18 = _____

5, 18, 1, 19, 5, 18 = _____

23, 1, 20, 3, 8 = _____

3, 15, 13, 16, 21, 20, 5, 18 = _____

A = 1	**H** = 8	**O** = 15	**V** = 22
B = 2	**I** = 9	**P** = 16	**W** = 23
C = 3	**J** = 10	**Q** = 17	**X** = 24
D = 4	**K** = 11	**R** = 18	**Y** = 25
E = 5	**L** = 12	**S** = 19	**Z** = 26
F = 6	**M** = 13	**T** = 20	
G = 7	**N** = 14	**U** = 21	

Just for Fun!

LESSON A

This is my sister.

Language Goals: Introduce people; Identify people

That's my sister.

1a

Find these people in the picture. Match the words with the picture.

1. mother __c__

2. father ____

3. parents ____

4. brothers ____

5. grandmother ____

6. grandfather ____

7. friend ____

8. grandparents ____

9. sister ____

 1b Listen and look at the picture. In the word list above, circle the people the boy talks about.

1c **PAIRWORK**
Take turns talking about Dave's family.

Those are his brothers.

That's his sister.

2a Listen and ⟨circle⟩ the words you hear.

(mother)	father	sister	brother
grandmother	grandfather	friend	grandparents

2b Listen again. Match the names with the people in the picture.

1. Dave _a_   **3.** Anna ____

2. Hideki ____   **4.** Jeff ____

2c PAIRWORK

Student A, cover the names in 2b.
Ask about the people in the
picture. Student B, answer the
questions.

2d Change roles and practice again.

Is this Jeff?

**No, it isn't.
It's Pete.**

Grammar Focus

Is this your sister?	No, it isn't.	This is my friend.	These are my friends.
Is that your brother?	Yes, it is.	That is my brother.	Those are my brothers.

3a Fill in the blanks with words from the box.

isn't

brother

is

✔ sister

That's Anna and that's Paul.

Is she your
1. ___sister___ ?

Yes, she
2. _____ .

And is he your
3. _____ ?

No, he
4. _____ .
He's my friend.

3b PAIRWORK

Practice the conversation with a partner.
Change partners and practice again.

3c

Write your brother's, sister's, or friend's name on the board. The other students guess who the person is.

Is Thomas your brother?

Is he your friend?

No, he isn't.

Yes, he is.

Thomas

4 GAME Scrambled Word Challenge

Scramble one of the words in the box.

Then write your scramble on the board. The other students guess the word.

mother	father
sister	brother
parents	grandmother
grandfather	friend
grandparents	

IS IT 'SISTER'?

RETSIS

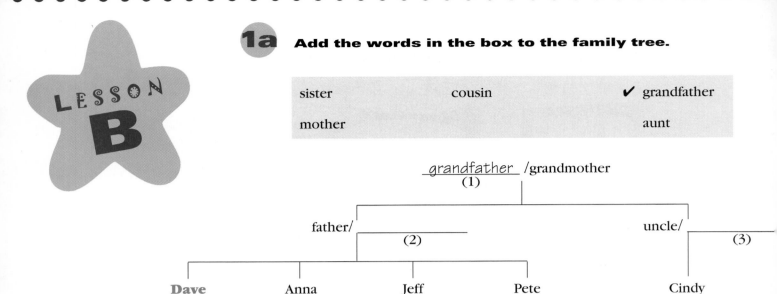

1a   Add the words in the box to the family tree.

sister	cousin	✔ grandfather
mother		aunt

<u>grandfather</u> /grandmother
(1)

father/ _____ (2)   uncle/ _____ (3)

Dave   Anna   Jeff   Pete   Cindy
              _____   (brother)   (brother)   _____
               (4)   (5)

1b   Draw a picture of your family. Then write family words *mother, father, sister, brother* on your picture.

2a   Listen and check (✔) the words you hear.

grandfather ____	grandmother ✔	cousin ____	father ____	mother ____
uncle ____	aunt ____	brother ____	sister ____	

Picture 1   Picture 2

2b   Listen again. Which picture are Dave and Hideki talking about?

2c   PAIRWORK

Tell your partner about your family. Use your picture from 1b.

These are my parents. This is my sister Anna. These are my brothers Jeff and Pete.

3a **Read the letter. Draw a picture of Emma's family.**

> Dear Maria,
>
> Thanks for the great photo of your family. This is my family. These are my grandparents, and this is my uncle. These are my two sisters and my brother. My sisters are Alice and Camille, and my brother is Evan.
>
> Your pen friend,
>
> Emma

3b **Complete the letter with the words in the box.**

brothers	parents	Nicky	✔ family

> Dear Teresa,
>
> This is my <u>family</u> . These are my <u>FAMILY</u> . And these are my _____ ,
>   (1)   (2)   (3)
> Tony and Bob. My sister is <u>good</u> .   Your pen friend,
>   (4)   Paul

3c **Write about your own family.**

4a **Bring a photo of your family to school and write a letter about it.**

4b **GROUPWORK**

Put the photo and the letter on the board. Put them in different places. The other students will match the photos and letters.

1 Key word check. Check (✔) the words you know.

this _____	that _____	these _____
those _____	mother _____	father _____
parents _____	sister _____	brother _____
grandmother _____	friend _____	uncle _____
grandfather _____	aunt _____	cousin _____
grandparents _____	she _____	he _____

2 Write five new words in your Vocab-builder.

3 Fill in the blanks with words from the unit.

Is _____ your sister?
(1)

Is this _____ brother?
(3)

These _____ my aunt
(5)
and uncle.

No, it _____. That's my sister.
(2)

No, _____ isn't. This is my cousin.
(4)

Those _____ my grandparents.
(6)

4 Fill in the blanks to spell two words from the unit.

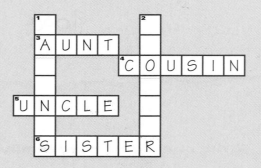

```
   ¹      ²
  ³A U N T
         ⁴C O U S I N
  ⁵U N C L E
  ⁶S I S T E R
```

Just for Fun!

Where's my backpack?

Language Goal: Talk about where things are

Where's my backpack?

Where are my books?

Where's my baseball?

It's under the table.

They're on the sofa.

It's in the backpack.

1

Match the words with the pictures.

1. table __e__

2. bed _____

3. dresser _____

4. bookcase _____

5. sofa _____

6. chair _____

7. backpack _____

8. books _____

9. keys _____

10. baseball _____

 1b Listen and number (1-5) the things in the picture when you hear them.

1c **PAIRWORK**

Practice the conversations in the picture. Then make your own conversations.

Where's the computer game?

It's under the bed.

2a **Listen and number these things (1–6) when you hear them.**

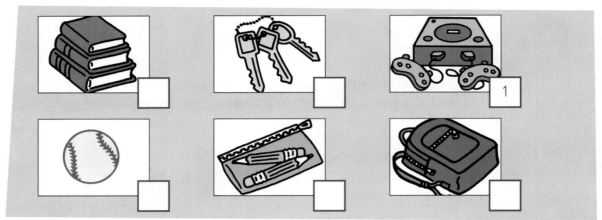

2b **Listen again. Where are the things from 2a? Number the picture (1–6).**

2c **PAIRWORK**

Ask and answer questions about the things in the picture.

Questions	Answers
Where's the baseball?	It's in the backpack.
Where is my computer game?	It's under the bed.
Where are your books?	They're on the chair.
Where are his keys?	They're on the dresser.
Where are her keys?	They're on the table.

Grammar
F o c u s

Put these sentences in order to make a conversation.

_____	I don't know.
_____	Is it on the dresser?
_____	No, it isn't.
1	Where's the bag?

3b PAIRWORK

Practice the conversation.

3c PAIRWORK

Look at the three pictures below.
Then ask and answer questions about the books, the keys,
the computer game, the pencil case, and the ruler.

4 GAME Find the Difference
PAIRWORK

Student A, look at the picture on page 19. Student B, look at the picture at right.

21

LESSON B

1a Match the words with the things in the picture.

1. math book __b__   **2.** alarm clock ____   **3.** CD ____

4. computer game ____   **5.** video cassette ____   **6.** hat ____

1b Look at Tommy's room for three minutes. Now close your books and write down all the things you remember.

1c PAIRWORK

Student A, ask
questions. Student B,
keep your book closed.

Where's the note-book?

It's on the bed.

2a Listen and circle the things Tommy wants from his room.

book	pen	pencil	CDs	ruler
notebook	video cassette	computer game	math book	

2b Listen again. Where are Tommy's things? Write notes.

The math book is on the dresser.

Dear Sally,

Please take these things to your brother: his math book, ruler, notebook, CDs, and video. The math book is on the dresser. The ruler is under the bed. The notebook is on the bed. The CDs are on the bookcase; the video is on the table.

Thanks, Mom

 Read the note and fill in the blanks in the chart.

On	math book
Under	

3b   **Look at the picture on page 22 and fill in the blanks with the words in the box.**

baseball	✔ hat	ID card	pencils
on the bookcase	on the table	on the floor	under the bed

Dear Sally,

Can you bring some things to school? I need my hat, my ID card, my pencils, and baseball. My ___hat___ is _on the bookcase_ . My _____ is
      (1)   (2)   (3)

_____ . My _____ are _____ , and my
  (4)   (5)   (6)

_____ is _____ .
  (7)   (8)

Thanks, Tommy

 3c PAIRWORK

Write a note to a friend asking for four things from your room. Say where they are.

4   GROUPWORK

Draw your ideal room. Then describe it to the class.

Here is my ideal room. My TV is on the desk. My telephone . . .

SELF CHECK ✔

1 Key word check. Check (✔) the words you know.

table _____	bed _____	dresser _____
bookcase _____	sofa _____	chair _____
backpack _____	books _____	keys _____
pencil case _____	baseball _____	hat _____
math book _____	alarm clock _____	CD _____
video cassette _____		computer game _____

2 Add five new words to your Vocab-builder.

3 Fill in the blanks with words from this unit.

Where _____ my backpack?   _____ under the table.
            (1)   (2)

Where _____ my keys?   _____ on the dresser.
            (3)   (4)

4 Unscramble these letters to spell words in this unit.

Example: balet = ___table___   **4.** neclip = _____

1. faso = _____   **5.** sreders = _____

2. koobs = _____   **6.** raich = _____

3. seky = _____   **7.** redun = _____

Just for Fun!

LESSON A

Do you have a soccer ball?

Language Goals: Talk about ownership; Make suggestions

Do you have a baseball bat?

Yes, I do.

Do you have a baseball?

No, I don't.

1a

Match the words with the things in the picture.

1. tennis racket ___c___

2. baseball bat _____

3. soccer ball _____

4. volleyball _____

5. basketball _____

6. television _____

 1b **Listen and circle the words you hear.**

baseball bat   soccer ball   television

computer game

1c **PAIRWORK**

Ask and answer questions about the things in the picture.

Do you have a baseball bat?

Yes, I do.

Do you have a baseball?

No, I don't.

2a **Listen to the conversation. Check (✓) the questions you hear.**

✓ **1.** Do you have a tennis racket?	**a.** Yes, I do.
____ **2.** Do you have a volleyball?	**b.** No, I don't.
____ **3.** Does he have a tennis racket?	**c.** Yes, he does.
____ **4.** Does she have a tennis racket?	**d.** No, he doesn't.
____ **5.** Do you have a baseball glove?	**e.** Yes, she does.
____ **6.** Do you have a soccer ball?	**f.** No, she doesn't.

  2b **Listen again. Draw lines from the questions you hear to the correct answers.**

2c **PAIRWORK**

Student A, ask your partner the questions in 2a.
Student B, close your book and answer the questions.

Grammar FOCUS

Do you have a TV?	Yes, I do.	No, I don't.
Do they have a computer?	Yes, they do.	No, they don't.
Does he have a tennis racket?	Yes, he does.	No, he doesn't.
Does she have a soccer ball?	Yes, she does.	No, she doesn't.
Does Chi-Young have a baseball?	Yes, he does.	No, he doesn't.

3a Fill in the blanks with words from the box.

soccer	let's	have	✔ don't

Let's play baseball.

No, I 1. _don't_ have a ball.

2. _____ play tennis.

I don't 3. _____ a tennis racket.

Well, let's play 4. _____ .

That sounds good.

3b PAIRWORK

Make conversations with your partner. Talk about the pictures below.

A: Let's play soccer.

B: I don't have a soccer ball.

A: Well, let's play volleyball.

B: That sounds good.

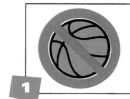

1

2

3

4a GROUPWORK

Write what you have in your bag. Don't write your name.

I have three books, a key, five pens, and a pencil case.

4b Exchange notes. Can you guess who wrote your note?

4c Tell the class what you learned.

Monica has three books, a key, five pens, and a pencil case.

LESSON B

1a **Match the words with the pictures.**

1. ✔ interesting ___c___ 3. fun _____ 5. relaxing _____

2. boring _____ 4. difficult _____

1b **Draw a picture of one of the words in 1a. Can your classmates guess what the picture is?**

 2a **Listen and check (✔) the words from 1a that you hear.**

 2b **Listen again. What does Tony say about these activities? Write a word from 1a in the blanks.**

Play computer games ___interesting___
(1)

Play volleyball _____
(2)

Watch TV _____
(3)

Play basketball _____
(4)

2c **PAIRWORK**

You are Tony. Your partner is Chi-Young. Talk about these activities.

Example: Chi-Young: Let's play computer games.

Tony: That sounds interesting.

Read this magazine article. Circle the sports things.

Ed Edgarson has a great sports collection. He has 70 tennis rackets, 39 basketballs, and 79 baseballs. He has 46 soccer balls and 32 volleyballs. But he doesn't play sports—he only watches them on TV!

3b **Look at the picture. Fill in the blanks in this magazine article about Sue Swanson.**

Sue Swanson has a small sports collection. She has five _baseballs_ , eight _____, four
              (1)   (2)
_____, and three _____.
    (3)   (4)
She plays sports every day!

3c **Write about sports things and other things you have.**

4 **SURVEY**

Write four questions with *Do you have?* Find people in the class who have these things. Write their names.

1. Do you have a sister?

Name: Chi-Young

2. Do you have a tennis racket?

Name: Manuel

3. Do you have a computer game?

Name: Tony

1 Key word check.
Check (✔) the
words you know.

basketball _____	tennis racket _____
baseball bat _____	baseball _____
soccer ball _____	volleyball _____
interesting _____	boring _____
fun _____	difficult _____
relaxing _____	television (TV) _____

2 Write five new words
in your Vocab-builder.

3 Fill in the blanks
with words from
the unit.

_____ you have a basketball?   Yes, I _____ .
  (1)   (2)

_____ Chi-Young have a tennis racket?   Yes, _____ does.
  (3)   (4)

Does Tony _____ a football?   No, he _____ .
             (5)   (6)

4 How many sports
can you name that
end in BALL?

____*base* ball   _____ ball   _____ ball

_____ ball   _____ ball   _____ ball

Just for Fun!

LESSON A

Do you like bananas?

1a

Match the words with the pictures.

1. hamburgers __d__

2. tomatoes ____

3. broccoli ____

4. french fries ____

5. orange ____

6. ice cream ____

7. salad ____

8. bananas ____

Language Goal: Talk about likes and dislikes

Do you like bananas? — 1 — *Yes, I do.*

No, I don't.

Do you like salad?

Yes, I do.

Do you like oranges?

1b
Listen and number the conversation (1–3) in the picture above.

1c PAIRWORK
Practice the conversations in the picture. Then make your own conversations.

Do you like oranges?

Yes, I do.

2a Listen and (circle) the foods you hear.

> (hamburgers)   tomatoes   broccoli   french fries
>
> oranges   ice cream   salad   bananas

2b Listen again and fill in the blanks.

2c PAIRWORK

Practice the conversation above. Give answers that are true for you.

Grammar Focus

Do you like salad?	Yes, I do.	No, I don't.
Do they like salad?	Yes, they do.	No, they don't.
Does he like salad?	Yes, he does.	No, he doesn't.
Does she like salad?	Yes, she does.	No, she doesn't.

I like oranges.	I don't like bananas.
They like salad.	They don't like broccoli.
He likes hamburgers.	He doesn't like french fries.
She likes ice cream.	She doesn't like bananas.

3 PAIRWORK

**Student A looks at this page.
Student B looks at page 99.
Ask your partner questions.
Find out what Bill and Bob
like and don't like.**

Draw 😊 or ☹ in the chart.

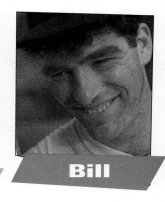

Bob

Bill

Chart for Student A.

	🍟	🍅	🥗	🥣
Bob	☹		😊	
Bill		😊		😊

4 GAME Do You Like...?

**Go around the class. Find students who
like these things. Write their names on
the picture. The first person to write
a name on each food is a winner.**

LESSON B

1a Write the number in the box next to the correct food.

1. broccoli	3. eggs	5. ice cream	7. banana	9. carrots
2. salad	4. apple	6. hamburger	8. orange	10. chicken

☐ ☐ ☐   ☐ ☐   ☐ ☐

☐

☐

☐

breakfast   lunch   dinner

1b **PAIRWORK**

How many other words can you add to the lists?

fruit: apples
vegetables: broccoli

2a Listen and circle the words from 1a that you hear.

2b Listen again and fill in the chart.

	likes	doesn't like
Katrina	apples	vegetables
Tom		

2c **PAIRWORK**

Ask and answer questions about what Katrina and Tom like and don't like.

Look at the breakfast, lunch, and dinner in activity 1a. Are they Katrina's or Tom's?

Write K or T

breakfast _____   lunch _____   dinner _____

3a Read the article below. <u>Underline</u> the fruits and (circle) the vegetables.

Runner eats well!

Middlebrook High running star Katrina Pedrosa eats lots of healthy food. For breakfast, she likes eggs, bananas, and apples. For lunch she likes hamburgers, salad, and oranges. And for dinner, she has chicken, tomatoes, french fries and, for dessert, ice cream.

3b Write about what Tom likes to eat for breakfast, lunch, and dinner.

For breakfast Tom likes eggs, oranges, and bananas. For lunch he likes ___hamburgers,___

_____ .

And for dinner he likes _____

_____ .

3c Write about what you like for breakfast, lunch, and dinner.

4a GROUPWORK

You are going on a picnic with a group of friends. Make a list of food to buy.

_____ LIST _____

bananas

4b Read your list of food to the class.

1 Key word check.
Check (✔) the
words you know.

apples _____	ice cream _____	salad _____
bananas _____	broccoli _____	like _____
oranges _____	carrots _____	breakfast _____
chicken _____	tomatoes _____	lunch _____
hamburgers _____	fruit _____	dinner _____
french fries _____	vegetables _____	

2 Add five new words
to your Vocab-builder.

3 Fill in the blanks.

Do you _____ broccoli?
  (1)

Yes, I _____ . / No, I don't.
  (2)

_____ they like fruit?
(3)

Yes, _____ do. / No, they don't.
  (4)

Does he _____ vegetables?
  (5)

_____ , he does. / No, he doesn't.
  (6)

_____ she like tomatoes?
  (7)

Yes, she _____ . / No, she doesn't.
  (8)

4 Fill in the blanks
with words
for these fruits.

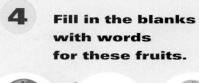

1   2   3

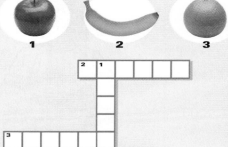

Just for Fun!

Do you like broccoli?

No, I don't.

Do you like carrots?

No, I don't.

Do you like ice cream?

Yes, I do.

Great! This is broccoli ice cream.

UNIT 7

How much are these pants?

1a

Match the words with the pictures.

1. socks __b__

2. T-shirt ____

3. shorts ____

4. sweater ____

5. bag ____

6. hat ____

7. pants ____

Language Goals: Ask about prices; Thank someone

How much is this T-shirt?

It's seven dollars.

How much are these socks?

They're two dollars.

 1b **Listen and (circle) the things in the picture you hear.**

How much are these shorts?

They're eight dollars.

1c **PAIRWORK**

Practice the conversations. Now ask about the other things.

37

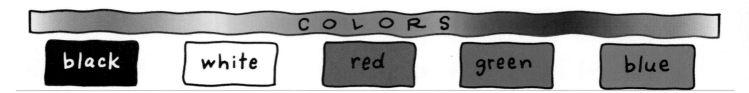

COLORS

black · white · red · green · blue

 2a **Listen to the conversations and ⟨circle⟩ the things in the picture you hear.**

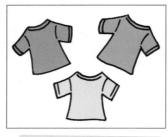

Conversation 1

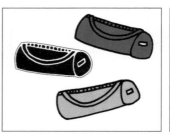

Conversation 2

Conversation 3

 2b **Put these words in order. Then listen again. Are you correct?**

1. A: much how T-shirt the blue is?
   How much is the blue T-shirt?

B: is ten dollars it.
_____

2. A: how black is bag the much?
_____

B: dollars seven it is.
_____

3. A: are red much the shorts how?
_____

B: they dollars nine are.
_____

 2c **PAIRWORK**

Ask and answer questions about the things in 1a.

How much are the green shorts?

They're eight dollars.

Grammar Focus

Questions	Answers	Look!
How much is the red sweater?	It's eight dollars.	It's = It is
How much is this blue T-shirt?	It's seven dollars.	
How much is that white bag?	It's nine dollars.	
How much are these black pants?	They're ten dollars.	They're = They are
How much are those blue socks?	They're three dollars.	

3a Fill in the blanks in the conversations.

How much is this
1. _____?

It's nine
2. _____.

I'll take it.

Here is your 3. _____.

You're welcome.

Thank you.

3b Practice the conversations above. Then talk about these things.

1. $8.00
2. $5.00
3. $6.00
4. $3.00
5. $10.00

4 GAME The Memory Game

Write a sentence. Then play a memory game.

Example: The blue sweater is seven dollars.

THE BLUE SWEATER IS $7.

THE BLUE SWEATER IS $7.
THE RED SOCKS ARE $2.

THE BLUE SWEATER IS $2?

NO!

 1a Listen and repeat.

| 10 | 11 | 12 | 13 | 14 | (15) | 16 | 17 | 18 | 19 | 20 |
| 21 | 22 | 23 | 24 | 25 | 26 | 27 | 28 | 29 | 30 | 31 |

1b Write a number from the box next to the correct word below.

ten _____   eleven _____   twelve _____   thirteen _____   fourteen _____

fifteen _____   sixteen _____   seventeen _____   eighteen _____   nineteen _____

twenty _____   twenty-one _____   twenty-two _22_   twenty-three _____   twenty-four _____

twenty-five _____   twenty-six _____   twenty-seven _____   twenty-eight _____   twenty-nine _____

thirty _____   thirty-one _____

 2a Listen and (circle) the numbers in 1a that you hear.

 2b Listen and (circle) the things in the picture that Lisa and her mom talk about. Check [✓] the thing Lisa buys.

2c PAIRWORK

Practice asking and answering questions about the clothes in the picture.

How much are the red socks?

They're $8.

3a Read the ad and fill in the price tags.

Mason's Clothing Store SALE

Come to Mason's sale for kids!

 $31.00

These bags are only $31.

Do you like sweaters? These are only $22.

And for girls, T-shirts in red, green, and black are only $11.

These socks are only $6.

3b Fill in the blanks in the ad with the words in the box.

Jackson's Clothing SALE

Come to Jackson's sale. Girls! These ___socks___ are only $4. These shorts
                                      (1)

_____ only $5. Do you like _____ sweater? It _____ only
   (2)   (3)   (4)

$15. For boys red, _____ , and blue T-shirts are only $10.
                        (5)

green
✔ socks
are
this
is

3c Use the information in this unit to write your own ad.

4 GROUPWORK

Write five questions about clothes. Then ask other students your questions.

1. Do you like blue?	5.
2. Do you have shorts?	6.
3. Do you like my green sweater?	7.
4.	8.

1 Key word check. Check (✔) the words you know.

2 Write five new words in your Vocab-builder.

3 Fill in the blanks to spell a word from the unit.

1. ____ WEATER   **4.** G ____ EEN

2. ____ AT   **5.** PAN ____ S

3. S ____ CKS   **6.** ____ HOES

bag ____	socks ____	shorts ____
sweater ____	T-shirt ____	black ____
blue ____	green ____	red ____
white ____	pants ____	how much ____
ten ____	eleven ____	twelve ____
thirteen ____	fourteen ____	fifteen ____
sixteen ____	seventeen ____	eighteen ____
nineteen ____	twenty ____	twenty-one ____
twenty-two ____	twenty-three ____	twenty-four ____
twenty-five ____	twenty-six ____	twenty-seven ____
twenty-eight ____	twenty-nine ____	thirty ____
thirty-one ____		

4 Fill in the blanks with words from the unit.

a. How _____ is this hat?   _____ $19.
   (1)   (2)

b. _____ much are these shorts?   _____ $22.
   (3)   (4)

c. How much _____ the blue sweater?   _____ $24.
   (5)   (6)

d. How much _____ the red socks?   _____ $15.
   (7)   (8)

e. Thank _____.   _____ welcome.
   (9)   (10)

Just for Fun!

LESSON A

When is your birthday?

1a
Listen and repeat.

MONTHS

1. January

2. February

3. March

4. April

5. May

6. June

7. July

8. August

9. September

10. October

11. November

12. December

Language Goal: Talk about dates

1b Listen and number the conversations in the picture.

1c **PAIRWORK**

Listen again and practice the conversations.

2a Listen and repeat.

1st	2nd	3rd	4th	(5th)	6th	7th	8th	9th	10th
11th	12th	13th	14th	15th	16th	17th	18th	19th	20th	21st
22nd	23rd	24th	25th	26th	27th	28th	29th	30th	31st

2b Listen and (circle) the numbers you hear in 2a.

2c Listen and match the names, months, and days.

Name	Month	Date
Lella	July	4th
Nick	August	22nd
Robert	January	5th
Jane	September	17th

2d PAIRWORK

Ask and answer questions about people's birthdays.

When is Leila's birthday?

Her birthday is September fifth.

Grammar Focus

Questions	Answers
When is your birthday?	My birthday is November 11th.
When is Leila's birthday?	Her birthday is September 5th.

3a PAIRWORK

Choose an ID and make a conversation.

> When is your birthday, John?
>
> It's March 21st.
>
> How old are you?
>
> I'm fifteen.

NAME: John Steward

DATE OF BIRTH: March 21st

AGE: 15

NAME: William Brown

DATE OF BIRTH: November 12th

AGE: 13

NAME: Leona Johnson

DATE OF BIRTH: June 3rd

AGE: 17

3b PAIRWORK

Practice again. Use your own name, age, and date of birth.

4 THE Birthday GAME

Ask the other students their birthdays and ages. Line up from the youngest to the oldest.

LESSON B

1 Match the pictures and the events. Write the correct letter next to the word.

1. _d_ speech contest   3. ____ school trip

2. ____ party ✔   4. ____ basketball game

a   b   c   d

2a Listen and check (✔) the events above that you hear.

2b Listen again and fill in Joe's calendar.

SEPTEMBER

24	25	26	27	28	29	30

OCTOBER

1	2	3	4	5	6	7
				Sally's birthday party		

2c PAIRWORK

Ask and answer questions.

When is Sally's birthday party?

It's October fifth.

3a PAIRWORK

Student A, read the student's schedule below.
Student B, read the student's schedule on page 99.
Then ask and answer questions to complete the schedule.

October

Basketball game	October 3
English speech contest	
Dave's birthday party	October 19
School trip	
Volleyball game	October 30

Joe, when is the school trip?

3b

Do you have these events at your school? Check (✓) the boxes.
Write the month, if you know it.

	yes	no	I don't know	month
School trip				
Speech contest				
Basketball games				

3c

What other events do you have at your school? Make a list.

4 GROUPWORK

Write five things about yourself on a piece of paper. Another student will read it to the class. Can your classmates guess who the student is?

I'm fifteen years old.
My brother's birthday is January 1st.
I like baseball and volleyball.

1 Key word check. Check (✔) the words you know.

2 Write five new words in your Vocab-builder.

3 Fill in the blanks with words from the unit.

birthday _____   date _____   month _____

January _____   February _____   March _____

April _____   May _____   June _____

July _____   August _____   September _____

October _____   November _____   December _____

school trip _____   party _____

speech contest _____   basketball game _____

When _____ your birthday?   _____ October 5th.
     (1)   (2)

_____ is his birthday?   It's _____ June 23rd.
 (3)   (4)

When _____ Sarah's birthday?   _____ birthday is August 15th.
     (5)   (6)

---

4 Unscramble these words.

astugu = _August_   daytirbh = _____   olcosh rpti = _____   ytpra = _____

yam = _____   berocto = _____   peches sottenc = _____   rilap = _____

Just for Fun!

LESSON A

Do you want to go to a movie?

1a

Match the kinds of movies with the posters.

1. action movie __a__

2. comedy _____

3. romance _____

4. thriller _____

Language Goals: Talk about preferences; Make plans

a **b** **c** **d**

Do you want to go to a movie?

Yes, I do. I want to see a comedy.

 1b **Listen and circle the kinds of movies in activity 1a you hear.**

1c **PAIRWORK**

Practice the conversation above. Then make your own conversation.

Do you want to go to a movie?

Yes, I do. I want to see an action movie.

2a Listen to Ben and Sally's conversation. Number the kinds of movies in the order you hear them.

_____ comedies	_1_ action movies
_____ romances	_____ thrillers

2b Listen again. In the chart, draw ☺ under the kinds of movies Ben and Sally like, and ☹ under the kinds of movies they don't like, and **?** for "I don't know."

	comedies	action movies	romances	thrillers
Ben				
Sally				

What kind of movies do you like?

I like action movies and comedies.

2c **PAIRWORK**

Ask and answer questions about the kinds of movies you like.

Grammar Focus

Singular	Plural
comedy	comedies
thriller	thrillers
action movie	action movies
romance	romances

Do you want to go to a movie?	Yes, I do./No, I don't.
Does he want to go to a movie?	Yes, he does./No, he doesn't.
Does she want to go to a movie?	Yes, she does./No, she doesn't.
What kind of movies do you like?	I like action movies and comedies.

3a Fill in the blanks with *and* or *but*.

I like thrillers and I like action movies.

I like thrillers but I don't like romances.

I like comedies
1. _____ I don't like action movies.

I like comedies
2. _____ I like action movies.

Brad　　**Maria**　　**Hideki**　　**Michele**

3b PAIRWORK

Take turns talking about the people in the picture.

Brad likes thrillers and action movies.

Maria likes thrillers but she doesn't like romances.

4 GAME Find Someone Who Likes . . .

Ask classmates what kind of movies they like.

Then find someone who likes the kinds of movies in the chart. Write his or her name in the chart. The first person to finish the chart wins.

What kind of movies do you like?

I like action movies and comedies.

Find someone who . . .	Student's name
likes comedies and thrillers.	_____
likes action movies but doesn't like romances.	_____
likes romances but doesn't like comedies.	_____
likes thrillers and action movies.	_____
likes comedies and romances.	_____

1a What kinds of movies are funny? Scary? Choose words from the box and write them under the pictures below.

| comedies | action movies | romances | thrillers |

1 scary

2 funny

3 exciting

4 sad
romances

1b **PAIRWORK**

Tell a partner what you think about the kinds of movies.

Romances are sad.

Action movies are exciting!

2a Listen and ⟨circle⟩ the description words in 1a that you hear.

2b Listen again. What kinds of movies do Eduardo and Jung Sook talk about? Fill in column 1. What words do they use to describe the movies? Fill in column 2.

	Kind of movie	Description
Eduardo	comedies	funny
Jung Sook		

2c **PAIRWORK**

Tell your partner what you think about movies.

Comedies are funny.

3a Read the movie review. Underline the words that tell us what the reviewer thinks about the two movies and the star of the movies.

Charlie Wayne is a great actor. And he has two new movies. *Listen in the Dark* is a thriller. It's exciting and it's scary. His other movie, *Crazy About You,* is a romance. But it isn't so great. In fact, it's boring.

3b Complete the movie review with the words in the box. Example:

Kevin Johnson is a great actor. His/her new movie is _Danger Zone_. It's an
(star of movie)   (name of movie)

action movie. The movie is _____exciting_____.
(kind of movie)   (description word)

boring

thriller

The Edge

Lorna Evans

1. _____ is not a great actor. His/her new movie is 2. _____.
   (star of movie)   (name of movie)

It's a 3. _____. The movie is 4. _____.
   (kind of movie)   (description word)

3c Now write your own movie review.

Anne Molovitch has a new movie. She is great. The movie is a romance. It is very sad.

Is it "Lost Love"?

4 **GROUPWORK**

Tell the group about a movie. Don't say the name of the movie. Your classmates guess the name of the movie.

UNIT 9 • Do you want to go to a movie? **53**

SELF CHECK

1 **Key word check. Check (✔) the words you know.**

action movie _____	comedy _____
romance _____	thriller _____
great _____	boring _____
scary _____	funny _____
exciting _____	sad _____

2 **Add five new words to your Vocab-builder.**

3 **Fill in the blanks with words from the unit.**

Do you _____ to go to a movie?
(1)

No, I _____ .
(2)

What kind of movies _____ you like?
(3)

I _____ thrillers.
(4)

What kind of movies _____ he like?
(5)

He _____ comedies.
(6)

4 **Make plurals.**

Example: movie ___movies___

1. comedy _____   **2.** romance _____   **3.** thriller _____

Just for Fun!

LESSON A

Can you play the guitar?

1a

What can these people do? Match the words and the people.

1. dance ___a___

2. swim _____

3. sing _____

4. play chess _____

5. paint _____

6. speak Spanish _____

7. play the guitar _____

Language Goal: Talk about abilities

I want to join the art club. ▢

Can you paint?

Yes, I can.

Can you swim? ▢

No, I can't.

I want to join the music club. 1

Oh, can you sing?

Yes, I can.

ART CLUB

SWIM CLUB

SPANISH CLUB

CHESS CLUB

MUSIC CLUB

 1b **Listen and number the conversations (1–3) in the picture above.**

1c **PAIRWORK**

Practice the conversations in the picture. Then make your own conversations.

I want to join the art club.

Can you paint?

2a **Listen to these two conversations and circle the clubs you hear.**

a. Spanish club

b. art club

c. music club

d. chess club

e. swimming club

What club do you want to join?

We want to join the chess club.

 2b **Complete the conversations with the words in the box. Then listen to the first conversation again and check your answers.**

to	club
want	✔ do
play	can't

Mario: What club ____do____ you want _____ join?
                      (1)   (2)

Lisa: We _____ to join the chess _____.
         (3)   (4)

Mario: Can you _____ chess?
               (5)

Lisa: No, I _____.
         (6)

Juan: I can.

2c **GROUPWORK**

Practice the conversation above. Then make your own conversation.

1   2   3   4   5

What club do you want to join?

I want to join the basketball club.

Grammar Focus

Can you dance?	No, I can't.
Can you sing?	Yes, I can.
Can he paint?	No, he can't.
Can she speak Spanish?	Yes, she can.
Can you speak Spanish?	Yes, we can.
Can they dance?	Yes, they can.

3a Put this conversation in order.

_____ I don't know.

_____ What can you do?

__1__ What club do you want to join?

_____ I can play the guitar.

3b Ask three students what they can do. Make a list and tell your class.

Example: A: What can you do?
B: I can play basketball.

Tom can sing. He can play basketball.

4 GAME I can do that!

On a piece of paper, write something you can do. Give the paper to your teacher.

Then make two teams. Each student takes a piece of paper and does the action. Students in the other team guess what you can do.

LESSON B

1a Match the words with the pictures.

drums __3__ piano _____ guitar _____ trumpet _____ violin _____

 1
 2
 3

 4
 5

1b PAIRWORK

Ask and answer questions about the instruments.

Can you play the piano?

No, I can't.

2a Listen and circle the words you hear.

| violin | sing | dance | trumpet |
| drums | piano | paint | |

2b Listen and fill in the chart with words in the box.

play the guitar	✔ sing
play the drums	play the piano
sing or dance	

	can	can't
Bill		sing
Jennifer		
Victor		

Can Bill play the guitar?

Yes, he can, but he can't sing.

2c PAIRWORK

Tell what Bill, Jennifer, and Victor can and can't do.

58

3a Read this advertisement from the school magazine. <u>Underline</u> the things they want people to do for the school concert.

Musicians Wanted for School Concert

Are you a musician? Can you <u>sing</u>? Can you dance? Can you play the piano, the trumpet, the drums, or the guitar? Then maybe you can be in our school concert. Please talk to Nick Tarantino for more information.

3b Complete the following poster with the words in the box.

guitar

can ✔

play

can

drums

sing

can

play

Musicians Wanted for Rock Band

We want two good musicians for our rock band. ____Can____ you
                                                 (1)

____ the ____ ? ____ you ____ ?
 (2)   (3)   (4)   (5)

____ you ____ the ____ ?
 (6)   (7)   (8)

Please call Liz at 790-4230.

3c Write your own poster for a sports day.

Wanted: baseball players
Can you play baseball? Please call Juan at 555-4779.

4 ## GROUPWORK

Ask your classmates what they can and can't do. Make a list.

Name	Can	Can't
Sally	dance	sing

1 Key word check. Check (✔) the words you know.

dance _____	swim _____	sing _____
play _____	chess _____	paint _____
speak _____	Spanish _____	join _____
music _____	art _____	club _____
violin _____	trumpet _____	drums _____
guitar _____	piano _____	can _____	can't _____

2 Add five new words to your Vocab-builder.

3 Fill in the blanks with words from the unit.

_____ you sing?
(1)

No, I _____ but I _____ dance.
(2)   (3)

Can she _____ Spanish?
(4)

No, she can't. But she can _____ the piano.
(5)

_____ he play the drums?
(6)

No, he _____ . But he _____ the guitar.
(7)   (8)

4 Find three words in the unit beginning with these letters.

C   _____   _____   _____

S   _____   _____   _____

P   _____   _____   _____

Just for Fun!

CAN YOU PLAY THE GUITAR?

What time do you go to school?

Language Goals: Talk about routines; Ask about times

1a

Match the words and the pictures.

1. go to school _a_

2. get up ____

3. run ____

4. eat breakfast ____

5. take a shower ____

What time do you usually get up, Rick?

I usually get up at five o'clock.

 1b **Listen and match the times and actions. Draw lines from the clocks to the pictures.**

1c **PAIRWORK**

One student is Rick. The other is the interviewer. Ask and answer questions about Rick's day.

What time do you run?

I usually run at six o'clock.

2a Listen to the conversation. Complete these sentences with words from the box.

two	one	two

Rick has _____ brothers and _____ sisters.
                   (1)   (2)

Rick's family has _____ shower.
                              (3)

2b Listen again and complete this shower schedule for Rick's family.

Time	Name
5:00	Alicia
	Rick
	Jerry
	Mary

When does Alicia take a shower?

She takes a shower at 5:00.

2c **PAIRWORK**

Ask and answer questions about when Rick and his brothers and sisters take showers.

Grammar Focus

What time do you get up?	I get up at six o'clock.
What time does he eat breakfast?	He eats breakfast at seven o'clock.
What time does she go to school?	She goes to school at eight o'clock.

3a Match the times and the clocks.

1. eleven o'clock   **a.**

2. six-fifteen   **b.**

3. eight-thirty   **c.**

4. nine-fifteen   **d.**

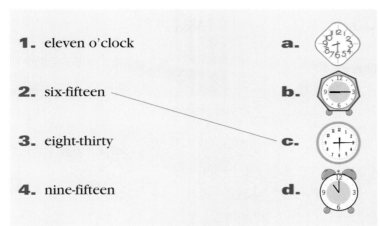

3b PAIRWORK

Ask and answer questions about the times. Cover the words in 3a and look at the clocks.

What time is it?

It's eight-thirty.

4 GAME The Bedtime Game

Walk around the room and ask the other students when they usually go to bed.

Then line up from the earliest to the latest bedtime.

I usually go to bed at eight o'clock.

I usually go to bed at eleven-thirty.

When do you usually go to bed?

1a When do people usually do these things? Match the actions and the time of day.

in the morning ___3___   in the afternoon _____   in the evening _____

1. do homework   2. eat dinner   3. eat breakfast   4. go to bed

1b PAIRWORK

Check your answers with another student. Do you agree?

 When do people usually eat dinner?

 People usually eat dinner in the evening.

 **2a** Listen and (circle) the activities you hear.

run	do my homework	(get up)
take a shower	eat dinner	go to school
eat breakfast	go to bed	eat lunch
go home		

 2b Listen again and write the times next to the actions.

1. gets up   ___5:00___   4. goes to school _____   7. eats dinner _____

2. runs   _____   5. goes home _____   8. goes to bed _____

3. eats breakfast _____   6. does homework _____

2c PAIRWORK

Ask and answer questions about Rick.

 When does Rick usually get up?

 He usually gets up at . . .

3a Read Jennifer's message to her pen pal and write down what she does at these times.

1. 6:15: ___gets up___   **2.** 7:30: _____   **3.** 8:00: _____

Dear Selina,

Thanks for your letter. Do you want to know about my morning? Well, I usually get up at around six-fifteen. I do my homework at six-thirty, and then I eat breakfast at around seven-thirty. At around eight o'clock, I go to school. School starts at nine o'clock. Please write and tell me about your morning.

Love, Jennifer

3b Complete the letter from Rick to his pen pal, José. Look at activity 2b for information about Rick's morning.

Dear José,

Do you want to know about my morning ? Well, I usually __get up__ at __5:00__ .
                                       (1)   (2)
At _____ I _____ , then I _____ at _____ .
   (3)   (4)   (5)   (6)
I _____ at _____ . Please write soon.
  (7)   (8)

Love, Rick

3c Write to Rick and tell him about your morning.

4 **GROUPWORK**
Ask the students in the class what they usually do in the morning.

When do you usually get up?

Around six-thirty.

1 Key word check. Check (✔) the words you know.

time ____	morning ____	breakfast ____
get up ____	go to bed ____	homework ____
clock ____	afternoon ____	lunch ____
run ____	watch TV ____	evening ____
dinner ____	eat ____	usually ____
o'clock ____	thirty ____	fifteen ____
take a shower ____	go to school ____	

2 Add five new words to your Vocab-builder.

3 Fill in the blanks with words from the unit.

What time _____ you eat breakfast?
        (1)

What time _____ Rick go to school?
        (3)

What time _____ she get up in the morning?
        (5)

I _____ breakfast at 7:30.
    (2)

He _____ at 8:00.
    (4)

She _____ at 6:30.
    (6)

4 Fill in the blanks and complete the crossword.

1. When do you get up in the _M_ _o_ _r_ _n_ _i_ _n_ _g_ ?

2. When do you come home in the _A_ _f_ _t_ _e_ _r_ _n_ _o_ _n_ _o_ ?

3. When do you go to bed in the __ __ _e_ __ __ __ __ ?

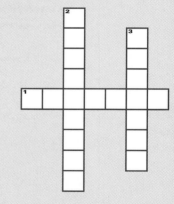

Just for Fun!

My favorite subject is science.

Language Goals: Talk about preferences; Give reasons

1a

Write the letters on the lines.

1. physical education (P.E.) _C_

2. art _____

3. science _____

4. music _____

5. math _____

1b

Listen and circle the subjects in 1a you hear.

1c PAIRWORK

Practice the conversation in the picture.
Then make your own conversation.

2a Listen and put the conversation in order.

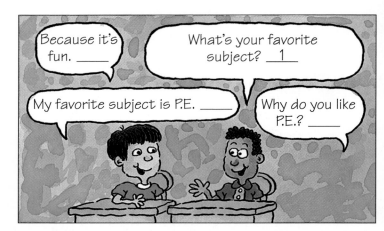

 2b Listen again to the complete conversation. Match the subjects and the description words.

Subject	Description Word
1. art	**a.** fun
2. science	**b.** interesting
3. music	**c.** boring
4. physical education (P.E.)	**d.** difficult
5. math	**e.** relaxing

2c What do you think? Write the number of the words from the first column next to the correct words in the second column.

2d **PAIRWORK**

Use the information in 2c to have a conversation.

What's your favorite subject?	My favorite subject is history.
What's his favorite subject?	His favorite subject is art.
What's her favorite subject?	Her favorite subject is P.E.
Why do you like math?	Because it's interesting.
Why does he like art?	Because it's fun.
Why does she like P.E.?	Because it's exciting.

3a Complete the conversation with the words in the box. You can use some of the words two times.

Who is your science teacher?

My science teacher is Mr. Baldwin.

teacher	my	subject	✔ your

A: What is ___your___ favorite _____?
    (1)   (2)

B: _____ favorite _____ is art.
    (3)   (4)

A: Who is _____ art _____?
    (5)   (6)

B: _____ art _____ is Mrs. Mendoza.
    (7)   (8)

3b PAIRWORK

Ask your partner about his or her favorite subject. Complete the chart below.

What is your favorite subject?

Who is your _____ teacher?

	Favorite subject	Teacher
Example	Art	Mrs. Mendoza
You		
Your partner		

4 GAME Question Challenge

Make two teams. Write ten sentences using the word "favorite."

Then read your sentences to the other team.
The other team makes up questions.

My favorite color is blue.

My favorite color is blue.

What's your favorite color?

LESSON B

1a Put these days into the correct order.

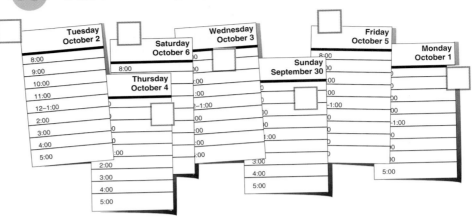

Tuesday October 2
Saturday October 6
Wednesday October 3
Friday October 5
Monday October 1
Thursday October 4
Sunday September 30

1b What subjects do you study at school? Check (✓) the subjects.

a. art
b. science
c. music
d. math
e. physical education (P.E.)

1c PAIRWORK

Ask and answer questions about the subjects you study at school.

When do you have math?

I have math on Monday, Wednesday, and Friday.

2a Listen. Write the school subjects you hear.

1. ___math___ 2. _____ 3. _____ 4. _____

2b Listen again and complete the chart.

	Favorite subject	**Why?**	**When?**
Ming	music	fun	Friday
Selina			
Ken			

2c PAIRWORK

Make conversations using the information in the chart.

What's Ken's favorite subject?

Science.

Why does he like science?

Because it's interesting.

3a **Read the following letter. Underline the school subjects Selina likes. Circle the subjects she doesn't like.**

Dear Jennifer,

It's Tuesday, November 11. I'm really busy today! At 8 o'clock I have math. I don't like (math.) Then at 9:00 I have science. It's difficult, but interesting. Next, at 10:00, I have history. It's boring, but at 11:00 I have P.E. That's my favorite subject! I eat lunch at 12:00. After lunch, I have music. Music is relaxing. I like my music teacher, Mr. Morgan. He's fun.

Love, Selina

3b **Complete Selina's schedule with information from 3a.**

Tuesday

Time	Subjects
8:00 to 9:00	
9:00 to 10:00	science
10:00 to 11:00	
11:00 to 12:00	
12:00 to 1:00	(lunch)
1:00 to 2:00	

3c **What is your favorite school day? Write your schedule for that day.**

4 **Ask the students in your class about their favorite days. Then tell your class what you learned.**

Steve's favorite day is Friday because he has art. He likes art.

Name	What's your favorite day?	Why?
Dave	Monday	Because I have music.
Steve	Friday	Because I have art.
Sarah	Tuesday	Because I play volleyball.

math _____	science _____	favorite _____
subject _____	Monday _____	Tuesday _____
Wednesday _____	Thursday _____	Friday _____
Saturday _____	Sunday _____	why _____
because _____	teacher _____	

physical education (P.E.) _____

1 Key word check. Check (✔) the words you know.

2 Add five new words to your Vocab-builder.

3 Fill in the blanks with words from the unit.

_____ your favorite subject?
(1)

My favorite _____ is science.
(2)

What's his _____ subject?
(3)

His favorite subject _____ art.
(4)

Why _____ you like math?
(5)

_____ it's interesting.
(6)

Why _____ he like art?
(7)

Because _____ fun.
(8)

4 Look at the alphabet chart. What do the numbers spell?

1, 18, 20 = ___ART___

19, 3, 9, 5, 14, 3, 5 = _____

13, 1, 20, 8 = _____

13, 21, 19, 9, 3 = _____

A = 1	**H** = 8	**O** = 15	**V** = 22
B = 2	**I** = 9	**P** = 16	**W** = 23
C = 3	**J** = 10	**Q** = 17	**X** = 24
D = 4	**K** = 11	**R** = 18	**Y** = 25
E = 5	**L** = 12	**S** = 19	**Z** = 26
F = 6	**M** = 13	**T** = 20	
G = 7	**N** = 14	**U** = 21	

Just for Fun!

LESSON A

Where is your pen pal from?

 1a

Listen and repeat these countries.

1. Taiwan

2. Korea

3. Japan

4. The United States

5. Australia

6. Mexico

7. Brazil

8. Argentina

9. The United Kingdom

Language Goal: Talk about where people are from

Where is your pen pal from?

He's from Brazil.

Where is your pen pal from?

She's from Taiwan.

 1b **Listen and (circle) the countries in 1a you hear.**

1c **PAIRWORK**

Practice the conversations in the picture. Then look at the things in your bag. Where are these things from? Ask and answer questions.

Where is your pencil from?

It's from Taiwan.

2a Where are these cities? Complete the chart below.

	City	Country
✔ Korea	Seoul	Korea
The United States	New York	
Brazil	Mexico City	
Mexico	Rio de Janeiro	
Japan	Tokyo	

 2b Listen and (circle) in 2a the cities and countries you hear.

 2c Listen again and complete the chart.

Name	City	Country
Juan	Tokyo	
Jodie		
Andrew		

Where is Juan's pen pal from?

He's from Japan.

Where does he live?

Tokyo.

2d PAIRWORK

Talk about the information in the chart.

3a

Look at the names of the countries in the box below.
What language do they speak in these countries?
Fill in the diagram.

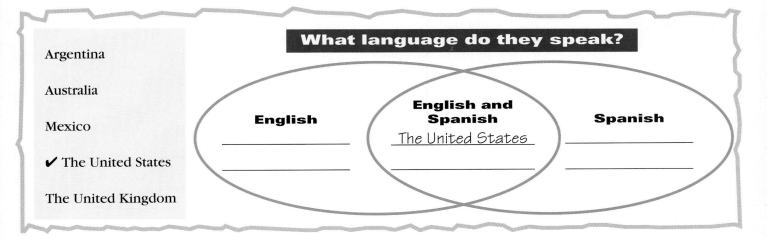

Argentina

Australia

Mexico

✔ The United States

The United Kingdom

What language do they speak?

English

_____

_____

English and Spanish

The United States

_____

Spanish

_____

_____

3b PAIRWORK

Choose a country and make a conversation.

This is my new pen pal. She's from Argentina.

What language does she speak?

She speaks Spanish.

4 QUIZ Name that Place!

In groups, write ten quiz questions.
Ask these questions of another group.

Q: Where is Rio de Janeiro?
A: Brazil

WHERE IS RIO DE JANEIRO?

IN THE UNITED STATES

NO! IN BRAZIL!

LESSON B

1 Match the countries and the languages.

SPANISH IN THIRTY EASY STEPS

PORTUGUESE IS FUN! | b |

JAPANESE FOR BEGINNERS

ADVANCED CONVERSATIONAL KOREAN

INTRODUCING WRITTEN CHINESE

OUR WORLD THRU ENGLISH

a. Taiwan
b. Brazil
c. Korea
d. Mexico
e. Japan
f. The United States

2a Listen and number the questions you hear.

| 1 | What's her name?

—— Does she have any brothers and sisters?

—— Where is she from?

—— Where does she live?

—— What's her favorite subject?

—— Does she speak English?

2b Listen again and write short answers to the questions [1–4] in 2a.

1.	Maria
2.	
3.	
4.	

2c **PAIRWORK**

You are Sophie. Your partner is Sophie's mom. Ask and answer questions about Sophie's pen pal.

Is that your new pen pal?

Yes, it is.

3a **Read this letter. Then write answers to the questions in the box.**

Dear Student,

My name is So-Young. I live in Seoul, Korea, and I want a pen pal in the United States. I'm 14 years old, and I speak Korean and English. I have a brother and two sisters. I like going to the movies with my friends and playing sports. My favorite subject in school is P.E. It's fun. Can you write to me?

So-Young

1. Where is So-Young from?   **3.** What languages does she speak?

2. What does she want?   **4.** What does she like?

3b **Complete this pen pal letter with the words in the box.**

✔ name	I'm	have	like	subject
write	live	want	in	speak

Dear Student,

My ___name___ is Tomoko. I _____ in Tokyo, Japan. I _____ a pen pal
        (1)   (2)   (3)
_____ the United States. _____ 17 years old. I _____ Japanese and
    (4)   (5)   (6)
English. I _____ a sister and a brother. I _____ music and dancing. My favorite
              (7)   (8)
_____ in school is English. Please _____ to me.
    (9)   (10)
            Tomoko Tamaguchi

3c **Write a letter to So-Young about yourself.**

4 **GROUPWORK**

Interview your partner. Make a list of questions. Ask your partner the questions. Then introduce your partner to the class.

This is Carmelita. She's from Brazil.

Taiwan _____   Korea _____   Japan _____   Mexico _____

Brazil _____   from _____   Seoul _____   New York _____

Tokyo _____   English _____   Spanish _____   Chinese _____

live _____   Korean _____   pen pal _____   Japanese _____

language _____   The United States _____   Argentina _____

Australia _____   Mexico City _____   Portuguese _____

The United Kingdom _____

1 **Key word check. Check (✔) the words you know.**

2 **Add five new words to your Vocab-builder.**

3 **Fill in the blanks with words from the unit.**

Where _____(1)_____ your pen pal from?   He's _____(2)_____ Korea.

_____(3)_____ is Juan's pen pal from?   He's _____(4)_____ Japan.

Where is her pen pal _____(5)_____ ?   She _____(6)_____ from Brazil.

Where _____(7)_____ he live?   He _____(8)_____ in Rio de Janiero.

_____(9)_____ does she live?   She lives _____(10)_____ Mexico City.

4 **Unscramble the names of these countries.**

1. DTNUIE TSATSE   **3.** WAITAN   **5.** LAZIBR

United States   _____   _____

2. AEROK   **4.** PANAJ

_____   _____

Just for Fun!

LESSON A

I'm watching TV.

Language Goal: Talk about what people are doing

1a

Match the words and the activities.

1. doing homework _d_

2. watching TV ____

3. cleaning ____

4. eating dinner ____

5. reading ____

(Speech bubbles in picture:)
- What are you doing?
- I'm watching TV.

1b

Listen. What are these people doing? Write numbers from 1a below.

a. Jenny _2_   **b.** Dave and Marie ____   **c.** Juan ____

1c PAIRWORK

Ask and answer questions about what people are doing in the picture.

(Speech bubbles:)
- What's he doing?
- He's reading.

2a Listen to the conversation and answer these questions.

1. What is Steve doing? _____

2. Does Steve want to go to the movies? _____

 2b Put these questions and answers in order to make a conversation. Then listen again. Are you correct?

_____ Do you want to go to the movies?

_____ I'm watching TV.

__1__ What are you doing?

_____ That sounds good. This TV show is boring.

2c **PAIRWORK**

Practice the conversation in 2b.
Then make your own conversations.
Talk about different activities.

What are you doing?

I'm reading a book.

Grammar Focus

Questions	Answers	Look!
What are you doing?	I'm watching TV.	
What's he doing?	He's doing homework.	what's = what is
What's she doing?	She's reading.	I'm = I am
		he's = he is
		she's = she is

3a Write the number of the picture next to the correct conversation.

Conversation A = _____

A: Do you want to go to the movies?

B: Sure, this video is boring.

A: When do you want to go?

B: Let's go at six o'clock.

Conversation B = _____

A: What are you doing?

B: I'm reading a book.

A: Do you want to go to the movies?

B: Sure, when do you want to go?

A: Let's go at 7:00.

3b PAIRWORK

Role play. Practice the conversations in 3a. Then look at picture 1 and make a conversation.

4 GAME The Mime Game

Use the words in 1a. Do an action.
The rest of the class will guess what you're doing.

1a Look at the pictures. Complete the chart.

	Places	Activities
1.		doing homework
2.	school	
3.		
4.		

swimming

pool

shopping

library

mall

playing basketball

1b PAIRWORK

Look at the chart in 1a.
Then ask and answer questions.

Where do people play basketball?

At school.

 2a Listen and and write the places you hear in the chart below.

 2b Listen again and complete the chart with the words in the box.

school	doing homework
mall	playing basketball
library	shopping

Name	Place	Activity
Tina	mall	
Mike		
Teresa		

2c PAIRWORK

Use the information in the chart to
have a conversation.

Hello, is Tina there?

No, she isn't. She's . . .

3a
Read the letter from Mike to his pen pal and <u>underline</u> the activities. Circle the places. Then read the letter again and number the photos [1–4].

Dear Sonia,

Thanks for your letter and the photos. Here are some of my photos. In the first photo, I'm <u>playing basketball</u> at (school.) In the second photo, I'm swimming at the pool. In the next photo, you can see my family at home. We're eating dinner. In the last photo, I'm with my sister Gina. She's doing homework—I'm watching TV.   Mike

1

3b
Fill in the blanks.

Dear Bob,

Here are some _____ . In the first photo, I'm _____ volleyball at school. In the second
        (1)   (2)

_____ , I'm _____ TV. And in the third photo, _____ doing homework.
    (3)   (4)   (5)

3c
Bring in some photos of your own (OR draw some photos of you and your family or friends!) and write about them.

This is a picture of me and my family.

4 GROUPWORK

Tell the group about your photos.

This is my brother, Scott.

He's playing soccer.

What is he doing?

SELF CHECK ✔

1 Key word check. Check (✔) the words you know.

eating _____   playing basketball _____

shopping _____   doing homework _____

reading _____   cleaning _____

watching TV _____   library _____

mall _____   pool _____

photo _____

2 Write five new words in your Vocab-builder.

3 Fill in the blanks with words from the unit.

_____ are you doing?
(1)

I'm _____ TV.
(2)

What _____ he doing?
(3)

_____ is doing homework.
(4)

What is she _____ ?
(5)

_____ is reading.
(6)

4 Write questions for these answers.

_____ ?   I'm watching TV.

_____ ?   That sounds good.

_____ ?   At five o'clock.

Just for Fun!

ARE YOU *SURFING?*   NO, I'M NOT.

ARE YOU *SWIMMING?*   NO, I'M NOT.

WHAT *ARE* YOU DOING?   I'M *WALKING!*

LESSON A
Where's the post office?

Language Goal: Ask for and give directions

1a

Match the words and the places in the picture.

1. post office ___f___

2. library _____

3. hotel _____

4. video arcade _____

5. bank _____

6. supermarket _____

7. street _____

8. pay phone _____

9. park _____

Is there a bank near here?

Yes, there's a bank on Center Street.

 1b Listen and ⟨circle⟩ the places in 1a you hear.

1c PAIRWORK

Practice the conversation in the picture. Now ask and answer questions about other places in the picture.

Is there a post office near here?

Yes, there's a post office on Bridge Street.

2a Match the sentences and the pictures. Write the number in the box.

1. The pay phone is across from the library.

2. The pay phone is next to the library.

3. The pay phone is between the post office and the library.

4. The pay phone is on Green Street.

2b Listen and fill in the blanks with the words in the box.

| next to |
| between |
| across from |
| on |

1. The library is ___between___ the video arcade and the supermarket.

2. The park is _____ the bank.

3. The supermarket is _____ Fifth Avenue.

4. The pay phone is _____ the post office.

2c PAIRWORK

Ask and answer questions about the places in 1a.

Where is the supermarket?

It's next to the library.

Grammar Focus

Where's the park?	It's on Center Street.
Where's the supermarket?	It's across from the bank.
Where's the pay phone?	It's next to the post office.
Where's the library?	It's between the video arcade and the supermarket.

3a Write the answers to these questions.

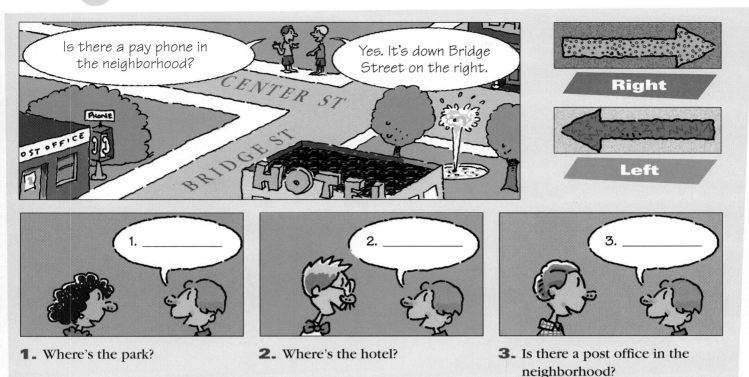

1. Where's the park?

2. Where's the hotel?

3. Is there a post office in the neighborhood?

3b PAIRWORK

Ask and answer the questions above.

4 GAME Ask me a question!

Take turns. Choose a place in the picture in 1a.
The other students ask questions and guess the place.

LESSON B

1a Match the words with the pictures below.

_e_ a clean park

____ a new hotel

____ a quiet street

____ a big supermarket

____ a dirty park

____ a small supermark

____ an old hotel

____ a busy street

1b PAIRWORK

Ask your partner about where he or she lives.

Is there a big supermarket near where you live?

Yes, there is.

2a Listen and ⟨circle⟩ the places in 1a you hear.

2b Listen again. Draw a map of Michael's neighborhood in the box.

2c PAIRWORK

Student A, say one true thing and one false thing about your map. Student B, say "true" or "false."

There is a big supermarket.

False! There is a small supermarket.

3a Read the tour guide and (circle) the description words. Underline the places.

Welcome to the garden district.

Turn left off (busy) First Avenue and enjoy the quiet streets and small parks of Windsor. Take a walk through the quiet park on Center Avenue. Across the street you will see an old hotel. Next to the hotel is a small house with an interesting garden. This is the beginning of the garden tour.

3b Complete the guide with the words in the box.

between	big	✔ busy
old	small	video arcade

Come and visit Bridge Street.

Bridge Street is a very ___busy___ street. There is a _____ supermarket.
         (1)   (2)

Across from the supermarket is an _____ post office and a big _____ .
                           (3)   (4)

_____ the post office and the video arcade is a _____ park.
  (5)   (6)

3c Write a guide to your town.

4 PAIRWORK

Tell a partner about where you live. Listen and draw a picture of where your partner lives.

My house is on a busy street.

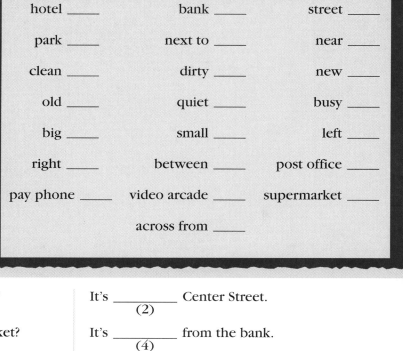

hotel _____   bank _____   street _____

park _____   next to _____   near _____

clean _____   dirty _____   new _____

old _____   quiet _____   busy _____

big _____   small _____   left _____

right _____   between _____   post office _____

pay phone _____   video arcade _____   supermarket _____

across from _____

1 Key word check. Check (✔) the words you know.

2 Add five new words to your Vocab-builder.

3 Fill in the blanks with words from the unit.

Where's _____ park?
(1)

_____ the supermarket?
(3)

Where _____ the pay phone?
(5)

_____ the library?
(7)

It's _____ Center Street.
(2)

It's _____ from the bank.
(4)

_____ next to the post office.
(6)

It's _____ the video arcade and the supermark[e]
(8)

4 Complete the crossword.

Down

1. A place to get money.

2. A place to have fun.

Across

3. A place to buy food.

4. A place to get books.

Just for Fun!

WHERE'S YOUR PHONE?

HERE

OH, NO!

IS THERE A PAY PHONE AROUND HERE?

LESSON A

Why do you like koala bears?

Language Goals: Describe animals; Express preferences

1a

Match the words and the pictures.

1. tiger _b_

2. elephant ____

3. koala bear ____

4. dolphin ____

5. panda ____

6. lion ____

7. penguin ____

8. giraffe ____

Let's see the pandas first.

Because they're very cute.

Why?

WELCOME TO THE ZOO

MAP

1b

Listen and check (✓) in 1a the animals you hear.

1c PAIRWORK

Make conversations about other animals. Use the words below.

cute   interesting   fun   smart

Let's see the lions.

Why do you want to see the lions?

Because they're interesting.

2a Listen. Write the animals you hear. Draw a line from the animals to the description words.

Animals	Description Words
1. ＿＿＿＿＿＿＿＿	**a.** interesting
	b. cute
2. ＿＿＿＿＿＿＿＿	**c.** fun
	d. smart

2b Listen and complete the conversation with the words in the box. You can use some words more than one time.

| very   dolphins   kind of   koala bears |

HE'S KIND OF BIG.

HE'S *VERY* BIG!

Julia: Let's see the ＿＿koala bears＿＿ .
(1)

Henry: Why do you like ＿＿＿＿＿＿＿＿ ?
(2)

Julia: Because they're ＿＿＿＿＿＿＿＿ cute.
(3)

Henry: Well, I like ＿＿＿＿＿＿＿＿ .
(4)

Julia: Why do you like ＿＿＿＿＿＿＿＿ ?
(5)

Henry: Because they're ＿＿＿＿＿＿＿＿ interesting.
(6)

2c **PAIRWORK**

Do you like these animals? Why or why not? Ask and answer questions. Use words from boxes 1, 2, and 3.

Box 1			Box 2	Box 3
tigers	dolphins	penguins	kind of	cute
elephants	pandas	giraffes	very	interesting
koala bears	lions			smart

Do you like giraffes?

Yes, I do.

Why?

They're very interesting.

Grammar Focus

Why do you like pandas?	Because they're very cute.
Why does he like koala bears?	Because they're kind of interesting.

3a Match the animals and the countries.

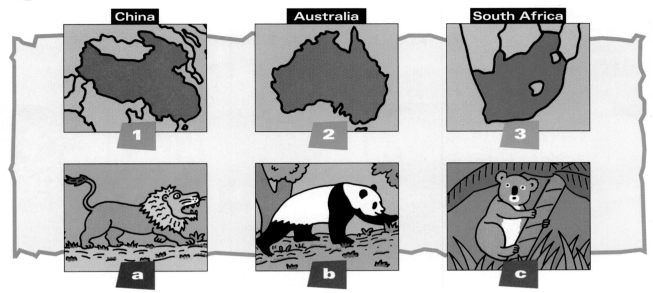

China **1**   Australia **2**   South Africa **3**

a   **b**   **c**

3b PAIRWORK

Practice with your partner.

Where are lions from?

Lions are from Africa.

4 GAME Bingo

Write nine of these words in the squares below.

Then listen and cross off (X) the words you hear.
Say BINGO when you get a row of Xs.
The first person to get a row of Xs in any direction is the winner.

penguins	Africa
dolphins	elephants
China	lions
koala bears	Japan
pandas	tigers
Australia	giraffes
Brazil	

Bingo!

LESSON B

1a Match the description words and the animals.

1. ugly _b_   2. intelligent _____   3. friendly _____   4. beautiful _____

5. small _____   6. cute _____   7. shy _____   8. scary _____

a

b

c

d

e

f

g

h

1b Talk about the animals you know.

I like penguins. They're beautiful.

 ## 2a Listen and (circle) the description words in 1a that you hear.

 ## 2b Listen again. Which animals do Tony and Maria talk about? What words do they use to describe them? Fill in the chart.

Animal	Maria's Words	Tony's Words

2c PAIRWORK

You are Tony. Your partner is Maria.
Say what you think about the animals.

Pandas are kind of shy.

Elephants are ugly.

3a Read the descriptions and match them with the animals below.

1. _____

Nellie

This is Nellie. She is twelve years old. She is from Africa. She likes to play with her friends and eat grass.

2. _____

Carla

This is Carla. She's five years old. She's from China. She's very beautiful, but she's very shy, so please be very quiet.

3. _____

Blinky Bill

This is Blinky Bill. Isn't he cute? He is from Australia. He sleeps during the day, but at night he gets up and eats leaves.

a

b

c

d

3b Look at the lion in 3a. Then complete the description with the words in the box.

he's years
✔ this eats
sleeps is

_____This_____ is Larry. _____ from Africa. He _____ eight
(1)   (2)   (3)

_____ old. He _____ meat. Larry is lazy. He usually _____
(4)   (5)   (6)

and relaxes 20 hours every day!

3c Write a description of another animal.

4 GROUPWORK

Exchange your description with other students.
Can students guess the animal?

It's a giraffe!

No, it isn't!

1 Key word check.
Check (✔) the
words you know.

panda _____	koala bear _____	giraffe _____
lion _____	tiger _____	dolphin _____
penguin _____	elephant _____	cute _____
friendly _____	ugly _____	intelligent _____
beautiful _____	shy _____	smart _____
Australia _____	China _____	Africa _____

kind of _____   very _____

2 Write five new words
in your Vocab-builder.

3 Fill in the
blanks with
words from
the unit.

_____ do you like penguins?
(1)

Why _____ he like tigers?
(3)

Why _____ she like elephants?
(5)

_____ they're very cute.
(2)

Because _____ kind of interesting.
(4)

Because they're very _____ .
(6)

4 Put the words in order so they make questions and answers.

Questions	Answers
elephants why like you do	intelligent because very are they
do like you why koala bears	cute kind of are they because
does she why dolphins like	because are they interesting

Just for Fun!

Additional Material

Additional material for Unit 2, Lesson B, activity 2c

Ask your partner about these things. Write the words in the chart below.

Is this her key?

No, it's his key.

pencil case

Student A

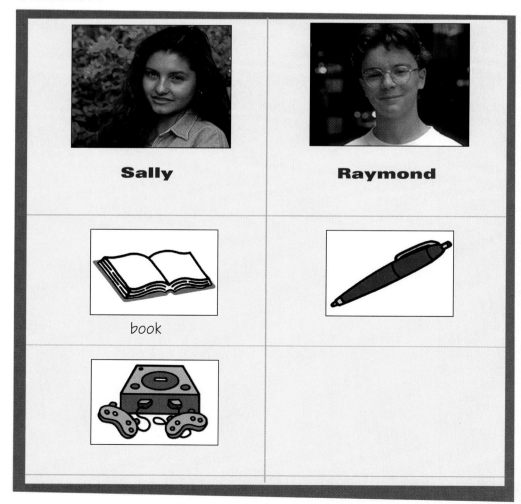

Sally

Raymond

book

Additional material for Unit 6, Lesson A, activity 3

Chart for Student B.

Bob		:(		:)
Bill	:)		:(	

Additional material for Unit 8, Lesson B, activity 3a

Schedule for Student B.

October

Basketball game	
English speech contest	October 7
Dave's birthday party	October 19
School trip	October 26, 27
Volleyball game	

Additional material for Unit 2, Lesson B, activity 2c

Ask your partner about these things. Write the words in the chart below.

Is this her key?

No, it's his key.

pen

Student B

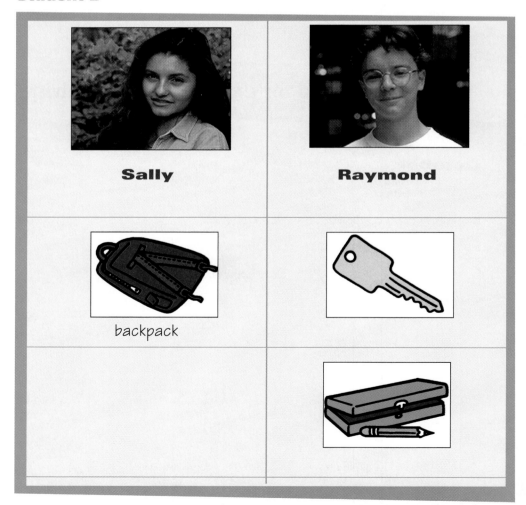

Sally

Raymond

backpack

Review
GAMES

How to Play the Game

1. **You need a die or something with the numbers 1 to 6.**

2. **You need counters.**

Rules

1. Each student has a counter.
2. Use the die to move your counter.
3. When you move to a new square, do the activity in the *Instructions Section*.

Instructions

1. **Look at the picture. Answer this question.**
   Where's the key?
2. **Spell your last name.**
3. **Introduce yourself.**
4. **Complete the answer.**
   Question: Is that your key?
   Answer: No, _____ _____ .
5. **Look at the picture. Answer this question.**
   Where's Tony?
6. **Complete the sentences.**
   _____ my brother. ___ my sister.
7. **Complete:**
   brother/sister
   uncle/_____
8. **Look at the picture. Answer this question.**
   Where's the backpack?
9. **Look at the picture. Complete the answer.**
   Question: Is Tony under the bed?
   Answer: No, _____ _____ .
10. **Ask for a student's phone number.**

11. **Look at the picture. Answer this question.**
    Where's the baseball?
12. **Complete the sentence.**
    My _____ and _____ are my parents.
13. **Look at the picture. Say the question.**
    Question: _____ _____ _____ _____ ?
    Answer: It's under the sofa.
14. **Look at the picture. Complete the question.**
    Question: _____ _____ the alarm clock?
    Answer: It's on the dresser.
15. **Complete the sentence.**
    This is my brother. _____ _____ my parents.
16. **Complete the answer.**
    Question: Is he your cousin?
    Answer: No, _____ my brother.
17. **Complete:**
    I/my
    she/_____
18. **Say the question.**
    Question: _____ _____ _____?
    Answer: I'm fine.

19. **Look at the picture. Complete the answer.**
    Question: Are his parents in the living room?
    Answer: No, _____ _____ .
20. **Complete the answer.**
    Question: Is his name Tony?
    Answer: Yes, _____ _____.
21. **Look at the picture. Say the question.**
    Question: _____ _____ _____ ?
    Answer: It's under the bed.
22. **Complete the question.**
    Question: What's _____ _____ ?
    Answer: I'm Tony.
23. **Complete the answer:**
    Question: I'm Mike.
    Answer: Nice __ _____ ___, Mike.
24. **Complete the question.**
    Question: What's _____ last name?
    Answer: My last name is Smith.
25. **Say the question.**
    Question: _____ _____ _____ _____ _____ ?
    Answer: D-R-E-S-S-E-R.

How to Play the Game

1. You need some counters.

2. Put a counter in the squares on page 105 when you ask or answer a question correctly.

3. Try to make a line of five squares.

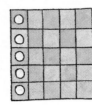 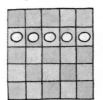 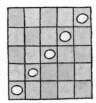

Instructions

1. Read about the information about the students below.

2. Ask and answer questions. Use the names at the top of the chart. Use a vocabulary idea on the left.

Gina
likes: soccer, hamburgers
doesn't like: basketball
birthday: June 1

Francisco
likes: TV, apples
doesn't like: tennis
birthday: March 23

Sarah
likes: tennis, oranges
doesn't like: baseball
birthday: September 3

Rita and Mary
like: green sweaters, ice cream
don't like: tomatoes

Kenji
likes: french fries, relaxing
doesn't like: chicken
birthday: October 13

Examples:

A: Does Gina like hamburgers?

B: Yes, she does.

A: Does Gina like basketball?

B: No, she doesn't.

A: When is her birthday?

B: Her birthday is June 1.

A: How much are the socks?

B: They're two dollars.

3. Put a counter in the square below.

Example:

A: Does Sarah like tennis?

B: Yes, she does.

These Are My Friends

	Gina	Francisco	Sarah	Kenji	Rita and Mary
Sports					
Food					
Clothing and colors					
Birthdays				FREE	
How much? $					

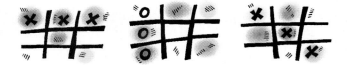
How to Play the Game

1. **Look at the information about Anna, George or your teacher. Ask and answer questions using the words in the box.**
2. **Put an "X" or an "O" in the box when you ask or answer a question correctly.**
3. **When you get 3 X's or O's in a row, you win.**

Questions and Answers ❀

Name:	Anna
Eats dinner:	6:00
Goes to bed:	11:00
Can:	dance
Likes:	funny movies
Favorite movie:	"Laughing Party"
Why:	because it's fun
Wants:	to go to a movie

she can dance	what's movie favorite her	eat when she dinner does
eat when she dinner does	go to bed time does she what	does want to go movie to a she
like she does movies sad	want she does dance to	like why "Laughing Party" she does

Name:	George	
Eats dinner:	6:00	
Goes to bed:	7:00	
Can:	run	
Likes:	school	
Favorite class:	math	
Why:	because it's interesting	
Wants:	to do his homework	

it what is time	eat breakfast time does he what	run want to does he
homework to do his want does he	his what's favorite class	school like he does
get when he up does	play chess can he	why math class like he does

My Teacher's Name _____

favorite movie his/her what's	first name his/her what's	play volleyball can he/she
time what eat dinner he/she does	that movie does why he/she like	when take a shower does he/she
can what do he/she	time he/she go to bed what does	swim can he/she

How to Play the Game

1. **You need a die or something with the numbers 1 to 6.**

2. **You need counters.**

Rules

1. Each student has a counter.
2. Use the die to move your counter.
3. When you move to a new square, do the activity in the *Instructions Section*.

Instructions

1. **Answer the question.**
   Is the library between the hotel and the video arcade?
2. **Answer the question.**
   Does Billy want to go swimming?
3. **Answer the question.**
   Is there a video arcade on River Street?
4. **Answer the question.**
   Where is Yoshi from?
5. **Ask the question.**
   No, there isn't a pay phone at the zoo.
6. **Look at Sarah. She's at the zoo. Ask the question.**
   Because she thinks they're cute.
7. **Ask the question.**
   It's next to the post office on Washington Avenue.
8. **Answer the question.**
   Does Yoshi speak Japanese?
9. **Answer the question.**
   Where's the school?
10. **Answer the question.**
    Does Billy's mother want to go swimming?

11. **Answer the question.**
    When does Anna want to go to the movies?
12. **Ask the question.**
    No, the supermarket's on Main Street.
13. **Ask the question.**
    Rita is in the park.
14. **Answer the question.**
    Is there a hotel in the neighborhood?
15. **Ask the question.**
    Yoshi speaks Japanese.
16. **Ask the question.**
    She's reading a book.
17. **Ask the question.**
    No, the video arcade isn't near the zoo.
18. **Answer the question.**
    Does Marie want to see the elephants?
19. **Answer the question.**
    Why does Marie like dolphins?
20. **Ask the question.**
    He lives in Osaka.

21. **Ask the question.**
    Where's _____?
    It's next to the video arcade.
22. **Ask the question.**
    He's playing tennis.
23. **Answer the question.**
    Is the hospital across from the library?
24. **Ask the question.**
    Let's go at 9:00.
25. **Ask the question**
    He's eating ice cream.

Vocab-Builder

On the lines below, write the words you learned in each unit

Unit 1

1.
2.
3.
4.
5.

Unit 2

1.
2.
3.
4.
5.

Unit 3

1.
2.
3.
4.
5.

Unit 4

1.
2.
3.
4.
5.

Unit 5

1.
2.
3.
4.
5.

Unit 6

1.
2.
3.
4.
5.

Unit 7

1.
2.
3.
4.
5.

Unit 8

1.
2.
3.
4.
5.

Unit 9

1.
2.
3.
4.
5.

Unit 10

1.
2.
3.
4.
5.

Unit 11

1.
2.
3.
4.
5.

Unit 12

1.
2.
3.
4.
5.

Unit 13

1.
2.
3.
4.
5.

Unit 14

1.
2.
3.
4.
5.

Unit 15

1.
2.
3.
4.
5.

Unit 16

1.
2.
3.
4.
5.

Vocabulary Index

Word Index—The numbers refer to where words first appear. For example, "ball" appears on page 25.

A

across from	p. 86
action movie	p. 49
Africa	p. 93
afternoon	p. 64
alarm clock	p. 22
alphabet	p. 9
am	p. 2
and	p. 50
apple	p. 34
April	p. 43
are	p. 20
Argentina	p. 73
art	p. 56
August	p. 43
aunt	p. 16
Australia	p. 73

B

backpack	p. 7
bag	p. 21
ball	p. 25
bananas	p. 31
bank	p. 85
baseball	p. 10
baseball bat	p. 25
basketball	p. 25
basketball game	p. 46
beautiful	p. 94
because	p. 68
bed	p. 19
between	p. 86
big	p. 88
birthday	p. 43

black	p. 38
blue	p. 38
book	p. 7
bookcase	p. 19
books	p. 19
boring	p. 28
Brazil	p. 73
breakfast	p. 34
broccoli	p. 31
brother	p. 13
busy	p. 88
but	p. 51

C

can	p. 55
can't	p. 56
carrots	p. 34
CD	p. 22
chair	p. 19
chess	p. 55
chicken	p. 34
China	p. 93
Chinese	p. 76
clean	p. 88
cleaning	p. 79
clock	p. 61
club	p. 56
comedy	p. 49
computer	p. 26
computer game	p. 10
cousin	p. 16
cute	p. 91

D

dance	p. 55
December	p. 43
difficult	p. 28
dinner	p. 34
dirty	p. 88
do	p. 26

does	p. 26
doesn't	p. 26
doing	p. 79
dollars	p. 37
dolphin	p. 91
don't	p. 26
dresser	p. 19
drums	p. 58

E

eat	p. 61
eating	p. 79
eggs	p. 34
elephant	p. 91
English	p. 75
eraser	p. 7
evening	p. 64
exciting	p. 52

F

family	p. 13
father	p. 13
favorite	p. 67
February	p. 43
first name	p. 3
found	p. 11
french fries	p. 31
Friday	p. 70
friend	p. 13
friendly	p. 94
from	p. 73
fruit	p. 34
fun	p. 28
funny	p. 52

G

get up	p. 61
giraffe	p. 91
glove	p. 26
go	p. 49

goes	p. 62
good	p. 27
grandfather	p. 13
grandmother	p. 13
grandparents	p. 13
great	p. 29
green	p. 38
guitar	p. 55

H

hamburgers	p. 31
hat	p. 22
have	p. 26
he	p. 15
hello	p. 1
her	p. 2
he's	p. 80
hi	p. 1
his	p. 2
history	p. 68
home	p. 83
homework	p. 64
hotel	p. 85
how	p. 10
how much	p. 37
how old	p. 45

I

I	p. 2
I don't know	p. 21
ice cream	p. 31
ID card	p. 5
I'm	p. 1
in	p. 19
intelligent	p. 94
interesting	p. 28
is	p. 2
isn't	p. 8
it	p. 8
it's	p. 4